HOW TO
RAISE KIDS
WHO WILL THANK YOU LATER
THE POWER OF EXPOSURE

RHONA J. VEGA

Copyright © 2026 by Rhona J. Vega
All rights reserved.
No part of this book may be reproduced, distributed, stored in a retrieval system, or transmitted in any form or by any means—electronic, mechanical, photocopying, recording, or otherwise—without the prior written permission of the publisher, except for brief quotations in reviews or scholarly works.

Scripture Notice
Scripture quotations in this book are taken from the Holy Bible, New International Version (NIV®).
Copyright © 1973, 1978, 1984, 2011 by Biblica, Inc.™
Used by permission. All rights reserved worldwide.

Disclaimer
This book is intended for informational and inspirational purposes only. The author shares personal experiences, insights, and perspectives related to parenting, education, and personal development. This book does not constitute legal, medical, financial, or professional advice. Readers are encouraged to seek appropriate professional guidance for their individual circumstances.

Editorial & Design Credit
Editing, interior design, and layout by The 1 and Only Publishing.

Publisher Information
Published by
The 1 and Only Publishing
4500 Forbes Blvd
Lanham, MD 20706
Email: info@the1andonlypublishing.com
Website: www.the1andonlypublishing.com

ISBNs
Paperback ISBN: 979-8-89741-043-9
eBook ISBN: 979-8-89741-044-6

Printing & Distribution
Printed in the United States of America.

This book is dedicated to my Queen Mother, Margaret Roberta Starks. You, mama, have been my entire world and inspiration. You modeled what intentional parenting was and I was watching every step of the way.

I miss you dearly but will forever continue your legacy.

Thank you mommy for loving me unconditionally and fiercely. Mostly thank you for reminding me to take lots of breaks to care for my own well-being so I could then be a better parent.

To my children and all the families we reach: I hope you will always follow the path of wisdom. Proverbs 22:6 reminds us to "Train up a child in the way he should go; even when he is old he will not depart from it."

ACKNOWLEDGEMENTS

Thank you God for my creation and for waiting all these years for me to figure out how to use the powerful gifts you bestowed upon me.

Thank you mama for raising me with so much love and support and for modeling and providing me with the best parenting blueprint.

You left me physically in 2020, but I feel your power and love every day protecting and guiding me. I think it's awesome that even though you raised us in public housing in New York City, you made us feel like we were wealthy and could literally be anything.

I love that you helped us raise our babies and gave them that same feeling, which guided me to birth an organization that continues to change lives today.

Thank you to my hubby and five children. Without the stability, foundation, and lived experience of raising brilliant Kings and Queens, none of this would be a reality. I'm grateful that I have lived long enough to watch you grow into amazing humans who will continue to make the world better than you found it. Thank you mostly for having the patience and love to put up with me, my creative ideas, and my spur of the moment family trips, and for giving me grace when I did everything wrong. I LOVE YOU more than you'll ever know.

Thank you to my amazing, supportive siblings, my phenomenal family, my Rock Star village, the Imagine Me Queens, my Sorors of Delta Sigma Theta, Inc., and everyone who has poured into me and my family.

A special thank you to all my children's educators and all the administrators who opened their doors to let us host Parent Matterz events at their school.

I'm super grateful to the Bergen County Youth Services Commission, The YWCA Northern New Jersey, The Teaneck and Englewood Public School Districts, and all involved in our Martha's Vineyard Youth Empowerment Expos over the years.

CONTENTS

Introduction 1

CHAPTER ONE:
The Power of Exposure 7

CHAPTER TWO:
You Can't Find Kids in a Database 29

CHAPTER THREE:
What No One Told Me About Parenting While Building 49

CHAPTER FOUR:
Evolving Our Parenting Legacy 69

CHAPTER FIVE:
College Readiness Isn't Just for Rich Privileged Kids 89

CHAPTER SIX:
Practical Dreaming, Career Exposure That Works 107

CHAPTER SEVEN:
The Blueprint for BIPOC Youth Empowerment 129

CHAPTER EIGHT:
Lost, Then Found—Guiding Teens Through an Identity Crisis ... 149

CHAPTER NINE:
From Exposure to Execution 169

CHAPTER TEN:
The Legacy Plan—Building Your Child's Future by Design 193

EPILOGUE:
Your Turn 213

Additional Resources 219

INTRODUCTION

Let me tell you something nobody told me when I was raising five kids on a budget:

Your child doesn't have to be exceptional to have exceptional opportunities. They don't need perfect grades. They don't need a trust fund. They don't need to be the smartest kid in the room or the star athlete or the one who "has it all figured out."

What they need is exposure.

And what you need is a plan.

I learned this the hard way—through trial and error, through sleepless nights wondering if I was doing enough, through moments when I felt invisible in spaces that weren't built for families like mine. I learned it by making mistakes, asking questions, and refusing to accept "No" when I knew there had to be another way.

Here's what I wish someone had told me twenty years ago:

The opportunities are out there. They're just not advertised to us.

The scholarships exist. The programs are running. The mentors are available. The colleges want diverse students. The doors are open.

But if you're waiting for someone to knock on your door and hand you a roadmap, you'll be waiting forever. Because the system isn't designed to find your child. It's designed to overlook them.

Not because your child isn't worthy. Not because they don't have potential. But because the families who already know the game have been playing it for generations. They know which programs to apply for in eighth grade. They know which summer camps lead to scholarships. They know how to navigate the college process, negotiate financial aid, and connect their kids to mentors who open doors.

And if you don't know those things? Your child gets left behind—not because they're not capable, but because nobody told you the rules.

That ends today.

This book is the roadmap I wish I had. It's the playbook I built while raising my own five children—each with different strengths, different challenges, and different dreams. It's the system I created after watching too many brilliant kids slip through the cracks because their parents didn't know what they didn't know.

My five children collectively received close to $1 million in college scholarships. Let me be clear: We're not rich. We're not connected to powerful people. We didn't have a trust fund or a legacy admission. What we had was strategy, persistence, and a refusal to let our circumstances limit our children's potential.

And I'm going to show you exactly how we did it.

But this book isn't just about college.

It's about raising children who believe the world is theirs to explore. It's about breaking cycles and building legacies. It's about making sure your child doesn't just survive—they *thrive*.

Because here's what I know after fifteen years of doing this work with hundreds of families through Parent Matterz: **Exposure is oxygen.**

When a child sees possibilities they didn't know existed, something shifts. When they meet someone who looks like them doing something they thought was impossible, the walls come down. When they step into spaces they were told weren't "for them," they start to see themselves differently.

Exposure doesn't just open doors. It changes belief systems. It interrupts limiting narratives. It plants seeds that grow into dreams your child didn't even know they were allowed to have.

But exposure without execution is just inspiration that fades. Your child can visit every college campus, attend every workshop, and meet every mentor—but if they don't know how to follow through, nothing changes.

That's why this book is structured the way it is. We're going to talk about exposure—how to find it, create it, and maximize it. But we're also going to talk about execution—how to turn opportunities into outcomes, how to coach your child through the hard parts, and how to build systems that actually work for your family.

Here's what you're going to learn:

You're going to learn how to find opportunities that most families never hear about—and how to position your child to access them.

You're going to learn how to build a village of mentors, advocates, and supporters who pour into your child when you can't be everywhere at once.

You're going to learn how to navigate the college process without losing your mind—and how to help your child graduate with as little debt as possible.

You're going to learn how to raise a child who doesn't just consume opportunities—they create them.

And you're going to learn how to do all of this while working full-time, managing a household, and trying not to lose yourself in the process.

Because let's be honest: This is hard.

Parenting is hard. Parenting while building a career is hard. Parenting while trying to give your child opportunities you never had? That's a whole other level.

But you're already doing it. You're already showing up. You're already fighting for your child's future in ways that nobody sees.

This book is here to make that fight a little easier. To give you the language, the tools, and the confidence to walk into rooms where you've never been welcome and demand a seat at the table for your child.

WHO THIS BOOK IS FOR

This book is for parents—and when I say parents, I mean all caregivers and overseers of young people—who are tired of watching other people's children get opportunities while yours get overlooked.

It's for you if you know your child is capable of more but don't know where to start.

It's for first-generation college navigators, first-generation business builders, first-generation "I'm-figuring-this-out-as-I-go" trailblazers.

It's for parents of Black, Brown, and marginalized children who are tired of systems that claim to serve "all students" but were never designed with your child in mind.

It's for working parents, single parents, overwhelmed parents—parents who feel like they're failing because they can't do it all.

It's for you.

WHAT THIS BOOK IS NOT

This is not a book about being a perfect parent. I'm not perfect, and my kids will tell you that in a heartbeat.

This is not a book about raising Ivy-League-bound prodigies. Some of my kids went to Ivy League schools. Some didn't. All of them are thriving because we gave them what they needed to succeed on their own terms.

This is not a book that promises easy answers or shortcuts. The work is real. The hustle is real. But so are the results.

And this is not a book that tells you to do it alone. One of the biggest lies we've been told is that good parents can do everything themselves. That's not strength. That's exhaustion. This book is about building systems and villages that carry your child when you can't.

HOW TO USE THIS BOOK

Each chapter is designed to give you both strategy and action. You'll read real stories—from my own family, from families I've worked with, and from students who've walked this path. You'll get practical tools you can implement immediately. And you'll get permission to do this imperfectly.

At the end of each chapter, you'll find action items. Don't try to do everything at once. Pick one. Do it. Then come back for the next one.

This is a marathon, not a sprint. And you don't have to run it alone.

MY PROMISE TO YOU

I promise you this: If you read this book, if you implement even half of what's here, if you refuse to let "I don't know how" stop you—your child's trajectory will change.

Not because I have magic answers. But because you'll have a roadmap. And a roadmap is powerful when you've been wandering in the dark.

I'm not going to tell you this will be easy. I'm going to tell you it's worth it.

Because twenty years from now, your child is going to look back and see that you didn't just wish for a better future. You built one.

Let's get to work.

Rhona J. Vega
Chief Dreamer of Parent Matterz
Mom of Five
Your Family's Story Success Coach

CHAPTER ONE
THE POWER OF EXPOSURE

It's not enough to tell kids they can be anything. They have to see it, touch it, hear it, and believe it's possible for them.

That's what exposure does. It interrupts limiting beliefs.

It widens the lens on what a child believes is possible—and it's the first step to building a future they'll thank you for.

Exposure is what helps a shy ninth grader realize she might be good at law after visiting a courtroom. It's what lets a junior who hates school discover he loves business after touring a sneaker factory. It's what turns a "C" student into a confident college freshman because someone took them to visit a campus before senior year.

When we talk about success, we tend to focus on outcomes: diplomas, jobs, test scores. But behind every success story is a moment of exposure—someone, somewhere, who opened a door and said, "Come see for yourself."

I've spent more than twenty-five years watching this transformation happen. I've seen kids who thought they had no future suddenly light up when they realized there was a whole world of possibility they'd never been shown. And every single time, it starts the same way—with exposure.

THE DAY EVERYTHING CHANGED FOR MY SON

My son was a high school sophomore who was only interested in sports and music. He wasn't overly excited about school, and honestly, academics weren't his focus. But I saw something in him—potential that needed the right environment to ignite.

I contacted a program focused on business and entrepreneurship and got him enrolled. In tenth grade, he attended a four-week program at The University of Pennsylvania (UPenn). That experience changed everything.

At UPenn, he discovered a newfound interest in business. His focus in school sharpened. But more than that, the exposure opened up his mind to careers, wealth-building opportunities, and entrepreneurship he'd never considered before. He entered business competitions alongside students from prestigious high schools—students from different socioeconomic backgrounds (though all students of color)—and he held his own. His confidence soared.

It was also where he learned what "summering in the vineyard" meant—a phrase that represented a whole world of privilege and opportunity he hadn't been exposed to before. That awareness didn't intimidate him. It motivated him.

From there, he received a tuition scholarship to college. He majored in finance in a small cohort on a Dean's scholarship. He continued his music, played internationally during college, and studied abroad. After graduation, he started his career in finance at Deloitte, and now works in finance at Sony.

Oh, and that YouTube channel he started in college? It's reached over 70,000 followers.

When I asked TV what that UPenn experience meant to him, he said it simply: **"Exposure is everything and can literally change your life!"**

EXPOSURE IS A STRATEGY, NOT AN EVENT

People assume exposure means bringing in a speaker or doing a field trip. But that's just the start.

Real exposure is about creating consistent access points to new environments, new voices, and new ways of thinking. It's about giving kids chances to try things, make mistakes, ask questions, and build confidence in spaces they never imagined themselves occupying.

It's also about disrupting assumptions. Too often, adults decide what kids are ready for based on grades or behavior. But I've seen kids with 2.0 GPAs run circles around 4.0 students when they're placed in the right environment. I've watched "problem students" become leaders when given meaningful responsibility. I've seen quiet kids transform into confident speakers after one semester of targeted exposure and mentorship.

The magic happens when we stop gatekeeping opportunities and start planting seeds—early, often, and with intention.

Think about it this way: If you've never seen a lawyer in action, how can you dream of becoming one? If you've never stepped foot on a college campus, how can you envision yourself there? If you've never met anyone who looks like you doing the work you're drawn to, how can you believe it's within your reach?

Exposure bridges that gap between "I wish" and "I can."

It takes abstract dreams and makes them tangible. It replaces vague aspirations with concrete next steps. It transforms hope into strategy.

WHY EXPOSURE MATTERS MORE THAN EVER

We're living in a time when information is everywhere, but access is still limited. A child can Google "what does a marine biologist do" and get a million results. But that's not the same as meeting a marine biologist, hearing their story, asking questions, and seeing yourself reflected in their journey.

The exposure gap—the difference between kids who've been shown what's possible and kids who haven't—is one of the most significant predictors of future success. And it has nothing to do with intelligence or potential. It has everything to do with access and opportunity.

Let me be clear: Some kids are born with exposure built in. They grow up in homes where dinner table conversations include discussions about career strategy, networking, and professional development. They have parents who are doctors, lawyers, engineers, entrepreneurs. They spend summers at enrichment camps and college prep programs. They're surrounded by people who've already walked the paths they want to walk.

Other kids? They're just as smart, just as capable, just as driven. But they've never seen those paths. No one in their family went to college. No one in their neighborhood runs a business. They don't know what questions to ask, who to ask them to, or where to even begin.

That's the exposure gap. And if we don't close it, we're leaving potential on the table—massive, world-changing potential that our communities desperately need.

EXPOSURE MUST START AT HOME

The truth is, most schools don't have the capacity to do this well. That's not a dig—it's reality. With budget cuts, understaffing, and systemic barriers, many schools are doing their best just to meet the basics.

That means exposure has to start at home, in the everyday moments that add up over time. It's in the car ride conversations. It's in the questions we ask. It's in who we bring around our children.

When I was raising my five kids, I made it my mission to expose them to everything I could—even when I didn't have the money for fancy programs or private school tuition. I took them to the post office and explained how the mail system works. I brought them to the bank and had them watch me open an account. I introduced them to every professional I knew and asked those professionals to talk to my kids about their work.

One of my sons once asked me, "Mom, how do you manage to generate conversations with strangers out of thin air?" And I realized—people skills are exactly that. Skills. They can be taught, practiced, and refined. But kids don't develop those skills sitting at home. They develop them through exposure to real people, real situations, and real conversations.

When parents are intentional about connecting their kids to opportunity—no matter how small—it sends a powerful message: I believe in your future, and I'm going to invest in it.

That investment doesn't require wealth. It requires curiosity, consistency, and a willingness to say yes to opportunities, even when they feel inconvenient.

YOU DON'T HAVE TO BE RICH TO OFFER EXPOSURE

Let's shut this myth down right now: Exposure isn't expensive. You don't need money to introduce your child to excellence. You need curiosity and consistency.

Some of the most powerful exposure moments I've created for kids cost absolutely nothing. I've connected students with professionals over Zoom calls. I've arranged job shadow days through personal connections. I've brought speakers into schools who volunteered their time because they remembered what it was like to be a kid with a dream and no roadmap.

Here's what you can do with zero budget:

Go to your local library and attend a career talk. Most libraries host free events featuring local professionals, authors, and community leaders.

Watch YouTube videos of professionals sharing their "day in the life." Make it a family activity. Watch together, pause to ask questions, and discuss what stood out to your child.

Ask your cousin, the banker, to talk to your child about budgeting and financial responsibility. Ask your neighbor, the nurse, to explain what a typical shift looks like. Ask your coworker, the manager, to share how they got promoted.

Introduce your child to someone you admire and let them ask questions. Most people are honored to be asked and happy to share their story.

Take your child to work with you—even if it's just for an hour. Let them see you in your professional element. Let them hear how you talk to colleagues, how you solve problems, how you navigate challenges.

Visit college campuses. You don't need to schedule an official tour.

Just walk the grounds. Sit in the student center. Let your child imagine themselves there.

Attend community events—town halls, cultural festivals, neighborhood meetings. Let your child see how communities organize, advocate, and create change.

You'd be surprised how many people will say yes. Most professionals remember what it was like to be a young person trying to find their way. They want to help. They just need to be asked.

EXPOSURE BUILDS IDENTITY

When kids are exposed early and consistently, they don't just gain information—they gain language and identity.

They start saying things like:

"I think I want to be an architect."

"I met someone who's a marine biologist, and that sounds cool."

"My mentor said I'm good at managing people."

They begin to own their interests, strengths, and direction. They stop letting the world define them by zip code, GPA, or mistakes.

I've watched this transformation happen hundreds of times. A kid who used to introduce themself by saying, "I'm just a student" starts saying, "I'm interested in environmental science" or "I'm thinking about business management."

That shift—from passive observer to active participant in their own future—is everything.

Because here's the truth: Kids can't become what they can't see. But once they've seen it, once they've touched it, once they've talked to someone who's living it, suddenly it becomes real. It becomes possible. It becomes a goal they can work toward instead of a fantasy they hope for.

That's what we're after—not just readiness, but agency. Not just preparation, but ownership. Not just exposure, but empowerment.

THE EXPOSURE GAP IS REAL

Let's name this plainly: The exposure gap is a key reason some kids soar while others stall.

It's not that some kids are smarter. It's not that some kids work harder. It's that some kids were shown earlier.

They've seen college campuses before senior year. They've had dinner with business owners. They've sat in on court cases. They've toured hospitals, law firms, tech companies, and newsrooms. They know how to network, how to shake a hand, how to ask good questions, and how to follow up with a thank-you email—because someone taught them.

Meanwhile, other kids are just as capable, just as ambitious, just as talented. But they've never been shown what's possible. They've never had access to those experiences. They don't know what they don't know.

That's not their fault. That's on us.

We have to close the gap—not just with more programs, but with a mindset shift. We have to stop waiting for schools to do it. We have to stop assuming someone else will handle it. We have to take responsibility for exposing our own children and the children in our communities to the opportunities they deserve.

Exposure isn't optional. It's a lifeline. It's the difference between a kid who says, "I guess I'll figure it out" and a kid who says, "I have a plan."

HOW TO MAKE EXPOSURE A HABIT

Exposure isn't about grand gestures. It's about consistency. The more your child sees, the more they dream. The more they dream, the more they prepare. The more they prepare, the more they achieve.

Here's what I tell parents in every workshop I lead:

Make exposure a family rhythm. One new experience a month. That's it. It doesn't have to be elaborate. It just has to be intentional.

Talk about careers over dinner. Not just, "What do you want to be when you grow up?" Ask, "What problems do you want to solve?" Ask, "Who do you admire and why?" Ask, "What kind of impact do you want to have on the world?"

Let your child shadow you. Take them to work. Let them sit in on your meetings or calls (when appropriate). Let them see how you move through your professional life. Let them witness your problem-solving, your professionalism, your work ethic.

Create a Possibility Wall. Collect pictures, articles, and quotes that reflect your child's interests and tape them somewhere visible. Make their options tangible. Make their future something they can see every day.

Build a network on their behalf. Reach out to professionals in fields your child is curious about. Ask if they'd be willing to have a 15-minute conversation with your child. Most people will say yes.

Normalize trying new things. Encourage your child to join clubs, attend workshops, volunteer in different settings. Every new environment is exposure. Every new challenge is growth.

Celebrate curiosity. When your child asks questions, honor that curiosity. When they express interest in something, follow up. Show them that their dreams matter by taking them seriously.

Document the journey. Keep a journal or photo album of every exposure experience. Let your child see how much they've grown, how many doors have opened, and how far they've come.

WHAT EXPOSURE DID FOR MY KIDS

None of my five children had the same path. Some went to four-year colleges. Some took different routes. Some figured it out early. Some needed detours. But all of them were exposed to opportunity—on purpose, consistently, and with love.

I used every connection I had. I created moments. I placed them in rooms before they thought they were ready. I signed them up for programs they didn't know they wanted. I introduced them to people who challenged them to think bigger.

I didn't have money for expensive summer camps. But I had relationships. I had resourcefulness. I had determination.

One of my daughters spent a semester interning at a nonprofit. One of my sons attended a leadership program because I filled out an application on his behalf when he was too intimidated to do it himself. Another daughter got involved in community organizing because I brought her to a meeting and introduced her to a mentor who saw her potential.

Were they always excited about these opportunities in the moment? No. Did they sometimes resist? Absolutely. Did I make them go anyway? You bet, I did.

Because here's what I knew that they didn't know yet: Exposure creates options. Options create freedom. Freedom creates possibility.

And now? They're thriving in their own ways. They're independent, confident, purpose-driven adults who know how to navigate the world because I didn't wait for someone else to show them. I showed them myself.

Not because I had all the answers. Not because I had unlimited resources. But because I had a commitment: to never let them think small for too long.

THE RIPPLE EFFECT OF EXPOSURE

Here's something beautiful about exposure: It doesn't just benefit the child receiving it. It creates a ripple effect that touches everyone around them.

When one kid in a family gets exposed to a new opportunity and thrives, their siblings pay attention. When one student in a classroom returns from a meaningful experience transformed, their classmates take notice. When one young person in a community breaks through barriers, they become proof that it's possible for others.

I've watched this happen time and time again. A student attends one of my empowerment expos and goes home fired up. They tell their friends. Those friends tell their parents. Those parents reach out to me asking how they can get their kids involved. And suddenly, instead of helping one kid, I'm helping ten. Instead of impacting one family, I'm impacting a whole network.

That's the power of exposure. It multiplies.

Every time we expose a child to something new, we're not just opening a door for them. We're showing everyone watching that the door exists and they have permission to walk through it too.

WHEN EXPOSURE LEADS TO UNEXPECTED PATHS

Sometimes, exposure leads exactly where you'd expect. A kid interested in medicine shadows a doctor and decides to become a doctor. Simple. Straightforward.

But sometimes—often, actually—exposure leads somewhere unexpected. And that's not a failure. That's a win.

I've had students attend engineering workshops and discover they love teaching. I've had kids tour law firms and realize they're more interested in social work. I've had young people attend business conferences and come back saying, "I want to be an entrepreneur, not work for someone else."

Exposure isn't about pushing kids toward a predetermined outcome. It's about giving them enough information, enough experiences, and enough perspective to make informed choices about their own lives.

The goal isn't to turn every kid into a doctor or lawyer. The goal is to turn every kid into a person who knows what they want, why they want it, and how to get there.

Sometimes that path looks exactly like we imagined. Sometimes it takes surprising turns. Either way, exposure gave them the foundation to choose confidently.

BUILDING AN EXPOSURE PLAN FOR YOUR CHILD

If you're reading this and thinking, "Okay, I'm convinced. But where do I start?" I've got you.

Start by getting curious about your child's interests. What do they talk about? What do they gravitate toward? What makes them lose track of time? What questions do they ask?

Don't worry if their interests seem all over the place. That's normal, especially for younger kids. The goal isn't to narrow their focus too early. It's to explore widely so they can make informed decisions later.

Once you have a sense of their interests, start brainstorming exposure opportunities:

- Who do you know in related fields?
- What local organizations offer programs or tours?
- What online resources exist (TED Talks, YouTube channels, virtual tours)?
- What books, documentaries, or podcasts could introduce new perspectives?
- What volunteer opportunities exist in that area?

Then, commit to one exposure activity per month. Put it on the calendar. Treat it like a doctor's appointment—non-negotiable.

Track what you do. Keep a simple log of dates, activities, and your child's reactions. Over time, patterns will emerge. You'll notice what lights them up and what doesn't resonate. That information is gold.

Adjust as you go. Exposure is a dynamic process, not a rigid plan. As your child grows and their interests evolve, your approach should evolve too.

And most importantly: Don't do this alone. Build a village. Connect with other parents who are committed to the same goal. Share opportunities. Carpool to events. Create a group chat where everyone posts about upcoming workshops, free programs, and local resources.

When we work together, we multiply our impact exponentially.

THE CONVERSATION THAT CHANGED HOW I SEE EXPOSURE

At the Martha's Vineyard Youth Empowerment Expo (MV Youth Expo) hosted by Parent Matterz, I witnessed a powerful "aha moment"—not from another parent observing their child, but from a mother reflecting on her own assumptions.

The MV Youth Expo was a hands-on session designed to help families understand the college process, academic planning, and the critical role of mentoring and exposure in a young person's journey. After listening to presenters talk about readiness, effort, and support systems, she turned to me and said something I'll never forget: **"My son said it was like Wakanda."**

She explained: Black professionals in droves—happy, successful, sharing resources, mentoring youth, showing so much love. Her son had never seen anything like it. And neither had she, in that concentrated, intentional way.

But her bigger realization came when she admitted: **"I thought my son would just 'figure it out,' but today I realized he needs mentors and experiences that can guide him before he gets to college."**

Her struggle was believing that because her son had a supportive family and certain advantages, he would naturally navigate the college path with ease. But the workshop made it clear: **Success doesn't come from proximity; it comes from preparation.**

She realized her son needed:

- Mentors who could speak into his life beyond what he hears at home
- Exposure to different career fields so he could see what he actually wants, not just guess
- To take the SAT more than once—not assume that one attempt would be enough

It was a shift from believing "he'll be fine" to understanding "he needs structure, strategy, and support."

She left the workshop with a concrete plan:

1. Identify mentors in areas he was curious about—engineering, entrepreneurship, and digital media.
2. Register him for multiple SAT dates to build confidence and improve scores.
3. Get him into real-world opportunities—site visits, shadowing, internships, and enrichment programs where he could test out interests instead of choosing blindly.

And she followed through.

Her son's SAT scores improved after retaking the test. Through hands-on experiences, he discovered which fields energized him and which ones didn't. That clarity changed his motivation, his discipline, and his approach to school. He went on to study finance in college, create an app as a freshman, start building a business, and even take a YouTube personality he admired to dinner to learn and grow. His confidence is now unimaginable.

The lesson? **Exposure is not about privilege—it's about intention.**

You don't need a special network or a perfect plan. You just need to put your child in rooms where they can see what's possible. The right workshop, the right conversation, the right mentor can shift a young person's entire direction.

Don't gatekeep and limit your child's potential because you haven't been exposed. Exposure isn't exclusive—it's a choice every parent can make.

YOUR CHILD IS WAITING

Right now, your child has dreams they haven't spoken out loud yet. They have potential they don't fully understand. They have gifts waiting to be discovered, strengths waiting to be named, passions waiting to be ignited.

But they can't get there alone. They need you to be intentional. They need you to create opportunities. They need you to believe in their future enough to invest in it—not with money you don't have, but with time, energy, and creativity.

They need exposure.

So let's begin.

Let's commit to showing our children what's possible before the world tells them what's not. Let's give them access to people, places, and perspectives that expand their sense of what they can become. Let's close the exposure gap—one conversation, one introduction, one experience at a time. Because when we expose our children to possibility, we don't just change their future. We change the future of everyone they'll go on to impact.

That's the power of exposure.

And it starts with you.

ACTION ITEMS FOR PARENTS

1. Schedule an "Exposure Date" This Month

Take your child somewhere new—a college campus, a museum, a courthouse, a local business, a community event. The goal isn't just to go. It's to observe, ask questions, and debrief afterward. In the car on the way home, ask: "What stood out to you? What surprised you? What questions do you still have?"

2. Identify Three Adults You Know in Different Careers

Make a list of people in your network who work in fields your child has expressed interest in—or fields they've never considered, but might find fascinating. Reach out and ask if they'd be willing to have a 15-20-minute conversation with your child, either in person, by phone, or over Zoom. Most people will say yes.

3. Start a Career Curiosity Journal

Buy a simple notebook or create a digital document where your child writes down one new job, career, or profession they learned about each week. It can come from a conversation, a TV show, a book, or something they noticed in the community. Review it together monthly and discuss which ones spark the most interest.

4. Create a Possibility Wall in Your Home

Dedicate a space—a bulletin board, a section of wall, the fridge—to display images, quotes, articles, and ideas related to your child's interests and potential paths. Let them add to it. Let it evolve. Make their future visible and tangible.

5. Share Opportunities With Others

When you find free programs, workshops, tours, or events that offer exposure, don't keep them to yourself. Text your friends. Post in your family group chat. Share on social media. A rising tide lifts all boats. The more we share, the more kids benefit.

6. Ask Better Questions

This week, instead of asking "What do you want to be when you grow up?" try these:

- "What kind of problems do you want to solve?"
- "Who do you admire, and why?"
- "If you could spend a day following someone around at their job, who would it be?"
- "What are you curious about right now?"

Better questions lead to deeper conversations. Deeper conversations lead to clearer direction.

SHARE THE MIC

"**MY DAUGHTER WANTED** to be a marine biologist. I saw the United Youth Aviators program advertised on the news when she was 12, and I put her on the waiting list. I never told her, but I called every few months to let them know how well she was doing in school. My persistence prevailed after three years—she finally got in.

On our drive to the airport, she was not excited. She reminded me what her dream career was. But after she experienced her first flight in the program, everything changed. She researched and saw the salary opportunities—she was hooked. She also discovered that out of a million pilots, only 3% are Black. There are only about 300 Black female pilots, and she wanted to be part of the change.

Now she's a Presidential Scholar at Spelman College. She entered as a sophomore and has maintained a 4.0 GPA. She's been on the Tamron Hall show, filmed a Spectrum commercial in Portugal, and most recently became the first-ever Procter & Gamble ambassador for Spelman.

She's also being sponsored by Nike for their first-ever HBCU campaign. One of her highlights was flying to Martha's Vineyard with her instructor for the first-ever Youth Opportunity Expo hosted by Parent Matterz in 2023. We found Rhona Vega on Instagram and were excited to visit MV for the first time. In 2025, my daughter was one of the keynote speakers at the Expo alongside her four Black instructors. It was powerful.

How do I describe what exposure did for my child? It literally changed her life and all of our lives."

—Lakeema F., Parent
Learn more: https://www.kamorafreeland.com/pressfeatures

"My mom really made sure I put my all into applying for a high-performing public magnet high school. I was nervous, and honestly? I was half-expecting a nerd school full of uptight rich kids, but the other half of me was hopeful that I would at least find other students of color.

Within the first few months of being there, I not only met other students of color, but also students of color from my own town whom I had never met before. I ended up meeting my best friend during a class, and we clicked right away. I got roped into my school's BSU (Black Student Union)—thankfully—and I was able to find a community where I could relate to others and be myself.

That experience showed me that I wasn't alone and that no matter where I went, there were people I would meet who would help me grow and develop into the person I am today. Exposure didn't just open a door—it helped me find my people. Through my newfound confidence, I became an intern at Parent Matterz and a leader in several other organizations."

—Isaiah L.

Need support?
Book a Complimentary Discovery Call

https://calendly.com/parentmatterz/early-start
Consulting-Discovery-Call

CHAPTER TWO
YOU CAN'T FIND KIDS IN A DATABASE

THE HARDEST PART OF MY WORK ISN'T CREATING PROGRAMS. It's finding the kids who need them most.

Let me tell you something that keeps me up at night: Right now, in your neighborhood, there's a kid with incredible potential sitting at home with no idea that opportunities exist. Their parent doesn't know about the free SAT prep program at the library. They've never heard of the summer enrichment camp that's actively recruiting students from underserved communities. They don't know about the scholarship that could cover their entire college tuition.

And here I am—along with dozens of other program directors, nonprofit leaders, and youth advocates—with resources, connections, and opportunities, desperately trying to reach them.

But I can't find them in a database.

I can't perform a Google search for "talented students who need support." I can't pull up a list of families who would benefit from what we're offering. The kids who need us most are often invisible to the systems designed to help them.

This is the paradox that drives me crazy and keeps me fighting: The resources exist, but the pipeline is broken. And until we fix that pipeline, we're leaving too many kids behind.

THE DAY I REALIZED THE SYSTEM WAS FAILING

A local public high school alumni association provided a grant so Parent Matterz could deliver enrichment resources, mentorship, and speed networking opportunities to underserved youth in their school and community. We called the workshops "Blueprint to Success: Pizza with Professionals." We even secured the youngest Black pilot in America as a speaker.

We did everything "right" according to traditional outreach methods. We worked through the teachers. We used the school email system. Administrators supposedly sent text messages. We posted on social media. We put up posters. The school even did a robocall.

And nobody came.

Well, almost nobody. Attendance was devastatingly low.

What happened? Teachers and guidance counselors never responded to our emails—never even opened them—so they never shared the information with their students. I think maybe half of what administrators promised actually got done. And I get it—everyone is overwhelmed and busy. Now we're asking them to add something else to their already overflowing plates.

Over the years, as I've met parents in the community, they've told me they had no clue about the more than twenty events we hosted at night in the library—with food donated by sponsors. Soul food, at that.

The realization hit me hard: pure sadness. I feel this work is "oxygen parents didn't know they needed." But if they don't know it exists, it doesn't matter how life-changing it could be.

That experience fundamentally changed my approach. I recommended focusing on students as a captive audience during the day—at lunch, during advisory periods, through speed networking and youth empowerment expos held during school hours. My thinking was simple: If we light a fire under the kids, send info home to them and to parents electronically, a kid will bug their parents about getting connected.

Sometimes the best way to reach parents is through their children.

THE INVISIBLE FAMILIES

Here's what people don't understand about outreach: The families who need support the most are often the hardest to reach.

They're not on the Parent Teacher Associations. They're not checking the school website. They're not in the parent Facebook groups. They're working two jobs, managing family crises, navigating systems that were never designed with them in mind.

When you send a flyer home, it might not make it out of the backpack. When you post online, they might not see it because they're not following those pages. When you rely on guidance counselors to refer students, those counselors might be overwhelmed, underresourced, or simply unaware of which students would benefit most.

And then there are the families who are actively disengaged from the school system—not because they don't care, but because the system has failed them so many times that they've stopped expecting anything from it.

I've met parents who stopped going to parent-teacher conferences because every meeting became a complaint session about what their child was doing wrong, with no solutions offered.

I've met families who stopped responding to school communications because every call, every letter, every email was about a problem—never about an opportunity.

I've met kids who are brilliant, curious, and capable, but who've learned to keep their heads down and stay invisible because visibility in school means trouble, not recognition.

These are the families we're missing. These are the kids falling through the cracks. And no database can help us find them.

THE SYSTEMIC BARRIERS

Let's be honest about the barriers that keep kids from accessing opportunity. Some are systemic. Some are local. All of them are solvable—but only if we're willing to acknowledge them and get creative about solutions.

Barrier #1: Information Doesn't Flow Equitably

Schools send information home assuming it will reach parents. But what if parents work night shifts and aren't home when kids get back from school? What if the child has executive function challenges and papers never make it out of their backpack? What if the parent can't read English fluently and the flyer isn't translated?

Information is power. And when information doesn't flow equitably, opportunity doesn't either.

Barrier #2: Trust Has Been Broken

In communities that have been historically underserved, there's often deep mistrust of institutions—and for good reason. Families have been promised help before and been let down. They've been told their kids are "behind" without being given tools to catch up. They've been judged, talked down to, and made to feel inadequate.

So when someone shows up offering free programs and opportunities, the first response isn't excitement—it's skepticism. What's the catch? What do they really want? Is this another way of telling us we're not good enough?

Building trust takes time, consistency, and proof. You can't just show up once and expect families to believe you're there for the long haul.

Barrier #3: Transportation Is a Real Issue

You can have the best program in the world, but if a family can't get there, they can't access it. Public transportation may not run on weekends or evenings when programs are scheduled. Parents may not have cars. Kids may not be old enough to travel independently.

This isn't a small problem. It's the reason I started offering transportation to some of my events. It's the reason I bring programs directly into schools and community centers instead of expecting families to come to me.

If we want to reach kids, we have to meet them where they are—literally.

Barrier #4: The "Good Kid" Myth

Here's something that makes me furious: the assumption that only "good kids" deserve opportunities. I've heard it a hundred times from well-meaning educators and program coordinators:

"We want motivated students." "We're looking for kids with good grades and no behavioral issues." "We need students who will take this seriously."

I get it. Resources are limited. People want to invest in kids who seem like "sure bets."

But here's the truth: Some of the most brilliant, capable, creative kids I've ever worked with had discipline records, failing grades, and attitudes that drove their teachers crazy.

They weren't bad kids. They were bored kids. Frustrated kids. Kids who'd been told they weren't good enough so many times that they stopped trying.

When we only reach out to the "good kids," we reinforce the very inequities we claim to want to dismantle. We leave behind the kids who need us most—the ones who could be transformed by one opportunity, one mentor, one person who sees their potential and refuses to give up on them.

HOW I STARTED FINDING KIDS TO HELP

After that painful realization, I stopped waiting for families to find me through "official channels." I started showing up everywhere.

I spoke at every PTO/PTA school event where administrators would allow me to speak. I spoke at churches when invited. I talked to parents at sporting events and kids at tailgate parties.

I personally connected families to opportunities—and sometimes drove them there myself. I helped connect our local high school to a college in our town offering FREE engineering, STEM, and cybersecurity programs to underserved high school students from other towns—programs that had been running for more than twenty years that nobody knew about. I personally interviewed families and explained the commitment they needed to make. And yes, I drove students to programs—both locally and in NYC—when parents were afraid to let their high school kids navigate public transportation alone.

I built relationships with leaders who opened doors for hundreds of kids. One woman—a Queen in every sense of the word—led a summer college enrichment program for high school students of color. She introduced my daughter to opportunities at Cornell and Hampton Universities. Over the years, she helped thousands of high school students by creating programs from Stanford University to South Africa. She opened doors for four of my kids and countless students from Parent Matterz.

I went to unconventional places to find kids. One time, I showed up at a tailgate party before the first football game of the season. (And I am NOT a fan of football, by the way.) I grabbed a group of young men and started pitching a financial literacy program. When I mentioned the prestigious company hosting the workshops, one of them said, "I heard my dad mention that company before. Yo, we should do this." That's all it took. One sentence. One connection. One open door.

I followed up relentlessly, even when parents said no. One mother told me, "He doesn't even like school." I didn't give up. A couple of sessions into the program, she called me back, stunned. She said he wanted to buy suits and new dress clothes. His attitude was changing about school and life because of the people who looked like him—people running the program and mentoring the students. She was happily surprised that he was engaged, empowered, and more confident.

That's what grassroots outreach looks like. It's messy. It's personal. It's showing up in places people don't expect. And it works.

THE POWER OF GRASSROOTS CONNECTION

Here's what I've learned: The most effective outreach doesn't happen through official channels. It happens through people.

When a mother tells her neighbor about a program that changed her daughter's life, that's more powerful than any flyer.

When a coach recommends a summer opportunity to his players, they listen—because they trust him.

When a kid comes back from an empowerment expo fired up and tells his friends, "Yo, you gotta come to this," that's the best marketing in the world.

Grassroots connection works because it's built on trust, relationships, and proof. It's not some faceless organization sending a generic message. It's someone you know, who cares about you, who's seen something work and wants you to benefit too.

This is why I always tell parents: You are the outreach. Every conversation you have with another parent, every program you recommend, every opportunity you share—you're closing the gap. You're making sure another family doesn't miss out because they didn't know.

THE NEIGHBORHOOD CONTACT LIST

One of the most practical things you can do right now is create a neighborhood contact list. This isn't complicated. It's literally a list of names, numbers, and information about resources available to families in your area.

Start with what you know:

- Which schools in your area have strong programs?
- Which community centers offer free or low-cost activities?
- Which churches, mosques, or temples have youth programs?
- Which local businesses offer internships or mentorship opportunities?
- Which nonprofits provide tutoring, college prep, or career exposure?

Then start collecting contacts:

- Find the names and numbers of youth coordinators at those organizations.
- Identify coaches, teachers, and mentors who are well-connected.
- Note which parents in your network are plugged in to different communities.

Keep this list updated. Share it freely. Make it a living document that grows as your network grows.

When you hear about a new opportunity, add it to the list. When someone asks, "Do you know of any programs for kids interested in STEM?" you'll have an answer ready.

This is how we close the information gap. Not through databases and algorithms, but through human connection and shared knowledge.

WHEN YOU CAN'T FIND THE KIDS, CHANGE YOUR STRATEGY

If you're a parent, educator, or community leader trying to reach young people and you're not getting traction, here are some questions to ask yourself:

- Am I going where the kids actually are, or am I waiting for them to come to me?
- Am I speaking in language that resonates with families, or am I using institutional jargon that feels alienating?
- Am I building relationships with trusted messengers in the community, or am I trying to do everything myself?
- Am I making it easy for families to say yes (transportation, timing, cost), or am I creating barriers without realizing it?
- Am I reaching out to all kids, or am I only targeting the ones who are already succeeding?
- Am I following up consistently, or am I assuming one announcement is enough?

These questions can reveal where your strategy needs to shift. Often, the solution isn't to work harder—it's to work differently.

WHY THIS MATTERS SO MUCH

Every kid we miss is a lost opportunity—not just for that child, but for all of us.

That kid who never learned about the engineering program might have designed the next breakthrough in renewable energy.

That teenager who dropped out before anyone connected them to a mentor might have become the teacher who transformed an entire school.

That young person who never got the scholarship information might have been the doctor who revolutionized healthcare in underserved communities.

We can't afford to keep losing kids because our outreach systems are broken. We can't keep putting the responsibility on families to find opportunities when the deck is stacked against them.

We have to go get them. We have to build networks. We have to become the bridges.

And we have to do it now—because every day we wait is another day a kid grows up thinking opportunity isn't for them.

MY COMMITMENT

I've spent decades doing this work, and I'll spend the rest of my life doing it if I have to. Because I can't accept a world where a kid's future is determined by whether their parent happened to see a flyer.

I'm going to keep showing up in communities. I'm going to keep building relationships. I'm going to keep making calls, sending texts, and knocking on doors.

And I'm asking you to join me.

Not because it's easy. Not because you'll always see immediate results. But because somewhere in your neighborhood, there's a kid waiting—whether they know it or not—for someone to find them and show them what's possible.

You can be that person.

Let's go find them together.

ACTION ITEMS FOR PARENTS

1. Create Your Neighborhood Contact List or Your Village List

Start a document (digital or physical) that lists:

- Local schools and their key contacts (principals, counselors, coaches)
- Community centers and youth programs
- Churches/religious organizations with youth activities
- Local businesses that might offer internships or mentorship
- Nonprofits focused on youth development
- Libraries and their program coordinators
- Parks and recreation departments

Update it regularly and share it with other parents in your network.

2. Identify Three Trusted Messengers in Your Community

Who are the people kids and families trust? Think beyond teachers—coaches, barbers, nail salon owners, youth pastors, community elders, local business owners. Introduce yourself. Let them know you're looking for opportunities for young people. Ask them to keep you informed.

3. Start or Join a Parent Resource Group

Create a group chat, Facebook group, or email list with other parents committed to sharing opportunities. Set a norm: Whenever anyone finds a program, scholarship, workshop, or opportunity, they share it immediately with the group. Make it easy for everyone to stay informed.

4. Adopt a "See Something, Share Something" Mindset

Commit to this: Every time you learn about an opportunity, scholarship, program, or resource that could benefit young people, you will share it with at least three other families. Don't assume they already know. Don't wait for the "right time." Just share it.

5. Attend One Community Event This Month

Go to a community meeting, a youth sports game, a church service, a neighborhood festival—somewhere you'll meet other families. Introduce yourself. Exchange contact information. Start building relationships outside your immediate circle.

6. Reach Out to One "Hard-to-Reach" Family

Think of a family in your community that seems disconnected from resources—maybe a neighbor you rarely see, a parent who seems overwhelmed, a family new to the area. Reach out. Offer to share information about programs. Offer to carpool to an event. Be the bridge for someone else.

SHARE THE MIC

"**I HAD NO IDEA** Parent Matterz existed until my hairstylist told me about it. My daughter had been talking about wanting to be a doctor, but we didn't know where to start. Nobody in our family went to college. We didn't know about pre-med programs or what she needed to do in high school to prepare.

Miss Vega connected us with a mentor, helped my daughter find a summer internship at a hospital, and walked us through the whole college application process. If my hairstylist hadn't said something, we would have missed all of that. Now my daughter is pre-med at Rutgers. All because someone shared information that could have easily passed us by."

—*Tanya B., Parent*

"I coach youth basketball at a local high school. Miss Vega came to one of our games and introduced herself. She told me about her programs and asked if I'd help spread the word to my players and their families. At first, I thought, 'Yeah, sure, another program.' But she followed up. She came back. She showed up for our kids.

Now I don't just tell families about her programs—I personally drive kids to her events because I've seen what happens when they go. These kids come back different. They come back believing in themselves. That's what happens when someone actually cares enough to find you."

—*Coach Marcus T.*

"Before I connected with Parent Matterz, my daughter was struggling emotionally and academically, and I almost had a nervous breakdown. I didn't know which way to turn. I saw a flyer and reached out to Miss Vega.

Learning about IEP support made all the difference. She connected me to other support systems—Child Study Teams, therapists, psychiatrists, 504 plans, and IEPs. My child has changed completely since then. What I would tell other parents in similar situations is this: You are your child's strongest advocate. The school doesn't know everything. If you feel your child needs support, find it. Reach out to programs like Parent Matterz that will guide you. I am grateful beyond words."

—*S. Dandie, Parent*

"Rhona's kids were a year ahead of my son. We happened to meet at a town daycare, and later on, we crossed paths again because this woman was always volunteering, devoting herself to her community. I told her about my son's challenges, and she shared an opportunity to expose him to something big. I did not know the existence of these opportunities. Rhona is an inspiration. I even told other parents to follow her on social media. She is constantly seeking things for these kids. She might have five kids of her own, but she has touched so many more."

—*Alex C., Parent*

"I met Rhona at a Cool Boys Read event that our children attended. During our conversation, we discovered many things in common—most strikingly, that we each have five children. Rhona shared her family's journey and her efforts to find affordable enrichment, tutoring, and programs that expose young people to new interests, industries, and careers. Over time, her passion for helping parents and students navigate college preparation grew into Parent Matterz, and I watched the program take shape through her care and dedication.

Each of my children faced different challenges and goals. My daughter excelled academically but needed opportunities to develop public speaking and leadership skills. My son wanted to explore journalism and build leadership experience. The college application process—from essays to organizing schools and deadlines—was difficult for our family. My youngest is now beginning the college search and is working through many of the same challenges.

Rhona and Parent Matterz were invaluable to us. Rhona shared information about programs and scholarships, offered practical suggestions, and provided support when obstacles arose. Through Parent Matterz, my children gained access to meaningful enrichment and mentorship opportunities.

Had we not connected with Rhona and Parent Matterz, we would have missed many of these opportunities. These programs helped my children develop hard and soft skills and discover more about themselves. As a working parent juggling family and other responsibilities, having Parent Matterz gather and share vetted information dramatically reduced my stress and frustration. It lightened my load and helped our family make better choices.

Today, three of my children have graduated from college and are working in technology, media, and management. One is a college senior, and my youngest is a high school senior preparing to begin college. I am deeply grateful for Rhona's guidance and for Parent Matterz—their expertise, resources, and personal attention made a real difference in our family's college journey."

—*Michelle L., Parent*

"I don't recall exactly when I first met Miss Vega, as I was loosely aware of Parent Matterz from before. However, I felt the connection when I first presented to a group of students at her pilot program *Middle to Medical School*—her authenticity and hard work were evident.

We share a passion for exposing all children, especially children of color, to the possibilities of STEM learning. While our children have the capacity to excel, many are not provided the opportunity and resources to allow them to flourish in these areas.

It is hard for many to be what they cannot see. Exposure allows one to think big. I had challenges with my own son. He was smart and intelligent; however, not every child fits into a one-size-fits-all learning model. Some learn and interpret differently. Rhona and her Parent Matterz resources and community offered the support to help him succeed.

Rhona and Parent Matterz provide a plethora of resources to young people in the community—resources that the average student may not receive, including information about scholarships, educational programs, corporate internships, and mentoring opportunities. My son benefited directly through resources, support, and tutoring."

—*Dr. Traci B., OB/GYN*

Need support?
Book a Complimentary Discovery Call

https://calendly.com/parentmatterz/early-start
Consulting-Discovery-Call

CHAPTER THREE
WHAT NO ONE TOLD ME ABOUT PARENTING WHILE BUILDING

"MOM, YOU WERE ALWAYS PAWNING US OFF ON OTHER PEOPLE. It felt like you didn't want to be bothered with us."

Those words came from one of my children during a therapy session, and they broke my heart.

Not because they weren't true—in a way, they were. But because the truth was so much more complicated than what my child had experienced.

I wasn't pawning them off. I was building them a village.

But here's what no one tells you about parenting while building: Your children won't always understand what you're doing. They won't see the strategy behind your choices. They won't know how hard you're working behind the scenes. They'll just feel your absence.

And sometimes, even when you're doing everything right, it will feel wrong to them.

This chapter is for every parent who's trying to build something—a business, a career, a mission, a legacy—while also raising children who need you. It's for the working moms who feel guilty for not being a classroom parent. It's for the entrepreneur dads who miss bedtime because they're chasing a dream that will benefit the whole family. It's for everyone who's ever felt torn between their purpose and their kids.

You're not alone. And you're not failing.

But you do need to be intentional.

Another issue my child had led to the therapy session. And then, in the middle of processing that issue, she asked me something that stopped me in my tracks: "Mom, did you really want to be a mom?"

I felt confused. Of all the questions I expected, that wasn't one of them.

In that moment, I stayed silent so she could get everything off her chest. I knew if I interrupted, if I got defensive, if I tried to explain myself too soon, she'd shut down. So I just listened.

When she was done, I explained what I was actually doing—not pawning them off, but connecting them to amazing people who had information and resources I didn't have. I was building a village because I knew I couldn't be everything they needed. I was strategic about who I brought into their lives and why.

In that moment, she just listened. She didn't argue. She didn't agree. She just absorbed what I was saying.

That conversation taught me to understand what children are hearing by our words and actions. What I thought was clear—what I thought was obviously love and investment—wasn't landing that way.

The gap between my intention and their experience was real, and I had to own that.

By the time this conversation happened, they were almost grown. But it changed how I communicated from that point forward. I choose my words carefully now and ask questions to make sure there is understanding. I don't assume they know why I'm doing what I'm doing. I tell them.

Where is our relationship now? Wonderful. That conversation, as painful as it was, opened a door. It gave us language to talk about things we'd never named before. And it reminded me that even when you're doing your best, your children still deserve to understand your heart.

THE INVISIBLE LOAD OF PARENTING WHILE BUILDING

When you're building something while raising children, people see the building. They see the business launch, the career advancement, the community work.

What they don't see are the nights you stayed up until 2 a.m. working after the kids went to bed, the constant mental gymnastics of balancing schedules and needs, or the exhaustion of trying to be everything to everyone. They don't see the judgment from other parents who don't understand why you can't volunteer for every field trip, or from colleagues who think you're less committed because you have parenting responsibilities.

This is the invisible labor. And here's what makes it harder: There's no blueprint for this, especially for parents who are first-generation business owners or breaking new ground in their communities. You're figuring it out as you go, and sometimes your kids feel the impact of your learning curve.

THE WORKING PARENT GUILT IS REAL

If you're a parent who works—especially if you're building something beyond a 9-to-5—you've felt the guilt. Guilt when you miss the school play for a critical meeting. Guilt when you're on your phone during dinner managing a crisis. Guilt when your child asks, "Why do you have to work so much?"

The guilt is real. But guilt isn't always a sign you're doing something wrong. Sometimes it's a sign you care deeply about multiple important things and you're navigating the tension between them.

The question isn't, "How do I eliminate the guilt?" The question is, "How do I parent with intention even when I can't be present for everything?"

CREATING A VILLAGE ISN'T ABANDONMENT

When my child said I was "pawning them off," what they didn't understand was that I was strategically placing them with people who could pour into them in ways I couldn't.

I knew I couldn't teach my son about music the way a trained musician could. I knew I couldn't expose my daughter to certain professional spaces the way a mentor in that field could. I knew I couldn't be everywhere, do everything, and meet every need—so I built a village of people who could fill the gaps.

But here's the key: I had to communicate that to my children. I had to help them understand that every person I connected them with was an extension of my love for them, not a replacement for my presence.

Creating a village isn't about offloading responsibility. It's about expanding capacity. It's recognizing that your child needs more than you alone can provide—and that's not a failure. That's wisdom.

Susan has been one of many important village members for my children. She's married to my nephew, and I strategically brought her into my kids' lives knowing they'd receive certain messages better from her than from me.

When I saw an ad for the town's Youth Advisory Board, I knew it would be perfect for my daughter. But instead of pushing it myself, I asked Susan to tell her about it. My daughter listened, applied, and became a founding member. That taught me something powerful: Sometimes the best parenting is knowing when to let someone else deliver the message.

Susan also created Cool Boys Read, a summer enrichment program specifically for her sons and other boys in the community. From 2007 to 2016, our boys, including youth from several states, participated in reading competitions, wrote stories for anthologies, created short films, and took educational field trips. What Susan provided was structure and accountability around reading that I couldn't maintain while working full time. The impact? My sons stayed academically engaged during summers and developed a love for storytelling. Both my sons wrote about their experience in Cool Boys Read in their college essays.

Dr. Frank, a college counselor, became another critical village member. My children formed a relationship with him, and he guided them through the college application process with care and expertise. He didn't just help them get into college—he helped them understand what college could be for them. That kind of guidance changes trajectories.

Congresswoman Nikema Williams met my daughter at Spelman College and became a mentor who saw something in her that needed nurturing. She poured into her, believed in her, and opened doors. That's what a village does—it multiplies the investment you're making in your child's future.

These relationships didn't happen by accident. I sought them out. I asked for help. I facilitated connections. And I stayed grateful for every person who said yes to pouring into my children.

WORDS AND ACTIONS MATTER

Here's what I learned the hard way: Your children are always watching and interpreting. What you think is obvious—your sacrifice, your strategy, your love—may not land the way you intend.

You have to close the gap between intention and interpretation. That means naming what you're doing and why. It means asking questions to understand what they're hearing. It means not assuming they see your heart just because you're working hard.

After that therapy session, I started being explicit with my kids. When I connected them with a mentor, I explained why. When I enrolled them in a program, I told them what I hoped they'd gain. When I had to miss an event, I named what I was working toward and how it benefited our family.

I also asked questions: "How are you feeling about this?" "What do you need from me right now?" "Do you understand why I made this choice?"

Those conversations created clarity. They helped my children see me not just as a parent making decisions for them, but as a person trying to build something meaningful while loving them fiercely.

THE REST STORY

After the birth of my fifth child, I developed a neurological illness that left me unable to walk without assistance, stand, or even hold my baby. I was bedridden for months. I had to hire help I couldn't afford.

That season forced me to rest—not because I wanted to, but because I had no choice.

And here's what I learned: Rest saved my life.

A friend introduced me to Queen Josepha, a woman who became a lifeline to me and my family. When I had my fifth child, my body shut down. Thank God, through medication, prayer, holistic chiropractors, and rest, I recovered fully in six months. All my doctors said it was a miracle. But I know what really happened: My body had reached its limit after years of trauma, fatigue, and attempting to be superwoman—when that's not reality.

Queen Josepha cared for me, my newborn, and the rest of my family when I couldn't. She came at 6 a.m. when my husband left for work and stayed until 7 p.m. when he returned. She helped with the morning routine, prepared dinner, washed and ironed clothes, and kept the house clean. For two years, I had help—REAL HELP.

It was like mom heaven. And this was the first time I can say I fully enjoyed motherhood. Can you imagine? This was my fifth child, and I was just realizing what it felt like to go to the grocery store without children in tow. To work without being completely overwhelmed. To come home to a prepared meal and clean clothes. I felt like a true Queen.

All those years I'd been pretending to be superwoman. Let me tell you: She doesn't exist. And I almost lost my life due to stress and burnout trying to do everything myself.

I come from a long lineage of powerful southern Black women who literally worked from sun up until sun down, and I had adopted those same ways. But that's not normal. And you will be a better parent, person, spouse, and friend if you take care of yourself and adopt self-care into your parenting journey. Accepting help with household chores and mundane tasks didn't make me less of a Queen—it made me smarter and prolonged my life.

Fourteen years later, when my youngest entered high school, I gave myself permission to go on a 30-day solo cruise to celebrate a milestone birthday. My husband held down the fort and encouraged me to go. That trip taught me that motherhood should be cherished, not survived. That taking care of yourself isn't selfish—it's essential.

It was my first solo time since I'd left for college—no kids, no spouse. I was scared, but it was life-changing. The best part? Everyone survived while I was gone.

My mom made me laugh when she said, "You're back from Africa so soon?" She had no idea how much I wanted to truly stay. It was my first of many life-altering visits to the continent to come.

From that point on, I built rest into my life. Every six weeks, I take a break. I model for my children that your well-being matters, that rest is productive, that you can't build a legacy if you're running on fumes.

Two weeks after returning from that life altering trip, my beloved Queen Mom passed away from COVID-19. The grief, the loss, the reality of how short life is—it hit me hard. Over the past two decades, I've lost many friends (parents, under age fifty) and losing loved ones reinforced what I'd learned during my own health crisis: You cannot pour from an empty cup.

Now I travel and rest for all the days my mom and friends wanted to and couldn't. Now I rest intentionally. I take breaks. I protect my energy. And I teach my children and other parents to do the same.

THE MOM MANIFESTO / DAD DIALOGUE

One of the most powerful exercises I recommend to parents who are building while raising kids is to write a manifesto—a clear statement of your values, your vision, and your commitments. This isn't just for you. It's a document you share with your children, your partner, your support system. It's a way of saying, "This is what I'm doing and why. This is what I need. This is what I'm committed to."

My dear late friend, Pat Phillips Walser, used to tell parents something I'll never forget: "Manage your children's education like you manage your job—or actually, better." Pat and her husband, Dr. Ardie Walser, lived this philosophy. They created Math Adventure and Word Play, a phenomenal FREE tutoring program for anyone, K–12, available every Saturday for more than twenty years.

Pat passed away last year after battling a brief and sudden onset of cancer at far too young an age. But her legacy lives on in the thousands of children who benefited from her commitment.

Here's the thing: Programs like Math Adventure and Word Play exist in communities everywhere—hidden gems that most parents never hear about. Pat's manifesto was clear: Education is a priority, and access should be free. She didn't just believe it. She built it. She showed up every single Saturday for two decades.

That's what a manifesto does. It clarifies what you stand for and holds you accountable to it. It becomes the blueprint for how you show up—not just for your own children, but for your community.

Here's how to create yours:

- **Name your core values.** What matters most to you as a parent or community leader? Education? Exposure? Faith? Community? Write down three to five non-negotiables.
- **State your vision.** What are you trying to build for your family? What legacy do you want to leave? Be specific.
- **Acknowledge your limitations.** What can't you do alone? What support do you need? Name it honestly.

- **Identify your commitments.** What will you protect no matter what? Weekly family dinners? Bedtime routines? Quality time?
- **Communicate it.** Share your manifesto with your family. Let your children know what you're working toward and why. Let your partner know what you need.
- **Revisit it regularly.** Your manifesto isn't static. As your children grow and your circumstances change, adjust it.

QUALITY OVER QUANTITY

You've heard it before, but it's true: It's not about how much time you spend with your kids. It's about the quality of that time.

I wasn't a classroom parent. I didn't volunteer for every field trip. But I was strategic about the time I did have. When I was with my kids, I was present. I asked questions. I listened. I made memories.

And here's the trick: I built in non-negotiable rhythms. Every half-day that kids were dismissed early from school, I took off work. That was my time with them—no exceptions. Those afternoons became sacred. We'd get lunch, talk, run errands together, or just hang out. It wasn't extravagant, but it was consistent. And consistency is what kids remember.

WHY YOU CAN'T DO IT ALONE

Let's be clear: You cannot parent and build alone.

You need help. You need support. You need a village that includes family, friends, mentors, and community members who believe in what you're doing.

But here's the hard part: You have to ask for help. You have to admit you can't do it all. You have to release control and trust other people to show up for your children.

That's scary. But it's also necessary.

The parents who thrive while building aren't the ones who do everything themselves. They're the ones who build systems, recruit support, and create networks that catch their kids when they can't be there.

HOW TO BUILD YOUR VILLAGE

Building a village doesn't happen by accident. It requires intention. Here's how to do it:

- Identify what your child needs. Academic support? Career exposure? Emotional guidance? A role model?
- Look within your network first. Who do you already know who could pour into your child?
- Be specific in your ask. Don't just say, "Can you mentor my kid?" Say, "My daughter is interested in graphic design. Could you spend an hour showing her what you do?"
- Facilitate the connection. Set up the initial meeting. Follow up. Express gratitude.
- Let the relationship develop. Don't micromanage. Let your child and the mentor build their own rapport.

A WORD FOR SINGLE PARENTS

I need to speak directly to the single parents reading this.

You're doing the work of two people. And I see you.

I see you juggling school drop-offs and work meetings. I see you staying up late to help with homework after a full day at your job. I see you choosing between attending your child's game or picking up an extra shift. I see you carrying the mental load of every permission slip, every doctor's appointment, every college deadline—alone.

And I need you to hear this: You are not failing.

You're doing something extraordinary. You're showing up every single day for your child while also being the breadwinner, the caregiver, the chauffeur, the homework helper, the disciplinarian, the cheerleader, and the one who keeps it all together. That's not lazy. That's not barely getting by. That's heroic.

But here's what I also know: You can't do this alone. And you shouldn't have to.

For single parents, the village isn't optional—it's essential.

When I talk about building a village, I know some of you are thinking, "That sounds great, Rhona, but I don't have time to build a village. I'm barely keeping my head above water as it is."

I get it. But here's the truth: You don't have time to *not* build a village. Because without support, you will burn out.

The village isn't about adding more to your plate—it's about sharing the load so you can breathe. For single parents, building a village starts small: Identify one trusted adult who can step in occasionally to pick up your child from school, help with homework, or take them to a program when you can't.

When you ask for help, be specific. Don't say, "Let me know if you can help sometime." Say, "Can you pick up my son from basketball practice on Tuesdays?" Trade with other parents—find someone in your child's school or neighborhood and offer to carpool, swap babysitting, share responsibility.

I am forever grateful for Queen Charlotte in North Carolina and Queens Rose and Norlean in California. They, along with my mom and sister Queen Renee, were my fierce village keepers who helped me stay strong emotionally, financially, and mentally wherever I lived. They literally saved my life and straightened my crown when needed.

Here's what I learned: quality over quantity—always. You might not have as much time as parents with a co-parent at home, but what matters is that when you're with your child, you're present. And rest is not optional. I know it feels impossible, but rest isn't a luxury for single parents—it's survival. Find a way to rest.

You're not doing this alone—even when it feels like it. Somewhere in your community, there are people who want to support you. Your job isn't to do it all yourself. Your job is to be intentional, ask for help, and build a village—one person, one connection, one opportunity at a time.

Your child will not remember that you couldn't afford the expensive summer camp or that you missed a few games because you were working. They will remember that you fought for them. That you showed up. That you believed in their future enough to chase opportunities, build connections, and refuse to let circumstances limit their potential.

You're doing the work of two people. And you're doing it well. Keep going. You've got this.

WHAT YOUR KIDS WILL UNDERSTAND LATER

Right now, your kids might not get it. They might feel like you're choosing work over them. They might resent your absences.

That's okay. They don't have to understand it now.

But one day—when they're older, when they're pursuing their own dreams—they'll look back and see what you were really doing. They'll realize you weren't abandoning them. You were showing them what it looks like to pursue a calling. They'll appreciate that you didn't just tell them to dream big—you modeled it.

But in the meantime? Keep communicating. Keep connecting. Keep showing up in the ways you can. And trust that the seeds you're planting will bear fruit in time.

ACTION ITEMS FOR PARENTS

1. Write Your Mom Manifesto or Dad Dialogue

Set aside an hour this week to write your manifesto using the framework above. Once it's done, share it with your family. Have a conversation about it. Let your kids ask questions.

2. Schedule One Mentoring Connection for Your Child

Think about what your child needs right now—career exposure, academic support, a positive role model. Identify one person in your network who could provide that. Reach out this week and set up an initial meeting.

3. Have a "State of the Family" Check-In

Gather your family for a conversation. Ask: "How is everyone feeling about how we're balancing everything right now? What's working? What's not? What do you need more of from me?" Listen without defending. Take notes. Make adjustments.

4. Protect One Sacred Time This Week

Choose one time block this week that will be 100% dedicated to your children—no phone, no work, no distractions. Put it on the calendar and treat it as non-negotiable, like you would a work meeting.

5. Identify Your Support Gaps

Make a list of things you need help with to better balance parenting and building. Who can you ask? What systems can you put in place? What needs to change?

6. Schedule Rest

Look at your calendar and block out time for rest this month. Not "catch up on work" time. Not "run errands" time. Actual rest. Sleep. Stillness. Spa. Recharge. Protect it fiercely.

SHARE THE MIC

"**GROWING UP** with the creator of Parent Matterz as my mom was like being the first student to enroll in her program, before the name was even an idea. I used to be so mad thinking about how most kids could just play video games for a summer and do whatever, while we had to go to these programs to learn. Like, what? You're telling me I gotta learn 365 days a year? The one thing my mom will tell you about me is that I do not like school in any sense of the word.

That understanding shifted in me when I started to take my future a little more seriously. When I was no longer being told to enroll in programs, like in high school, I already found that sense of motivation that led me to apply for internships that would put me on the right trajectory.

As soon as I landed that Meta Software Engineering internship offer, the pieces fell into place, and I was able to build upon that ever since, all thanks to the several LONG applications, essays, summer programs, weekend programs that I didn't want to do then. But my mom had the foresight to know how much they would impact my growth in this world.

I'm more than grateful for these values that she's instilled in me, teaching me how to be an avid go-getter, how to make connections and keep them. As a Black man in a white world and not-so-diverse industry, you're gonna be faced with so many challenges. Getting set up in a position to succeed and perform well beyond 'their' benchmarks for you is something I will always be thankful for mom giving to me. Love you momma."

—*Seti V., Rhona's Baby Boy aka "My Tech Wiz"*

"I put my career on hold to raise my children. No regrets, but I know that my life would have gone in a different direction if I hadn't done this. No guilt, because I see how my children are doing, and I am so proud of them. I see it as a delay and not a denial. I am an empty nester, so I'm now pursuing my dreams.

I think my own drive to succeed has definitely spilled over into my children's lives. I want the best for them and, because I want them to succeed, I tried my best to expose them to the world, not only academically, but also through sports and travel. The one thing I tell parents is to be involved in their child's life. So many parents do not understand the importance of being involved. I see the difference it makes. Parent Matterz was crucial in my parenting journey."

—*Dr. Donna G. Parent*

"I am married to Rhona's nephew, so I have been in her children's lives since they were young. I remember seeing an ad about the town's newly formed Youth Advisory Board and thought it would be a great opportunity for her daughter. Rhona asked me to tell her about it directly, knowing the information would be better received coming from me. She applied, aced the interview, and became a founding member of the Youth Advisory Board. I was so proud of her!

From 2007 to 2016, Rhona's boys participated in Cool Boys Read, a summer enrichment program I created. The primary focus was to keep the boys reading during the summer to prevent learning loss.

They engaged in friendly competitions, wrote stories published in an anthology every year, created an original short film, and took educational field trips.

I think one of the things that Rhona has always done is to reach out to her village for support in parenting. She often says she didn't raise her kids alone, and she is keenly aware that her kids might respond better to the same advice she is giving if it comes from someone outside of her household. I think Rhona's kids know that there is a tremendous network of people who are invested in their success and well-being."

—*Susan H., Parent and Founder of Cool Boys Read*

"My mom works hard at an event planning job while also taking care of me and my brother and loving us. Before that, she worked at a record label. I don't feel bad about how busy she is because she finds a way to make time for us, and we like hanging out when we all get back from school or work, and on weekdays.

I wish she understood how much my brother and I love her, and sometimes we can make mistakes, but we don't mean any harm. I appreciate everything that my mom does for not only me but also my brother, family, and even her friends! She always makes sure we have what we need, and I'll make sure now and when I'm older that she is always taken care of."

—*Quincy M., Age Fifteen, Ninth Grade*

Need support?
Book a Complimentary Discovery Call
https://calendly.com/parentmatterz/early-start Consulting-Discovery-Call

CHAPTER FOUR
EVOLVING OUR PARENTING LEGACY

The first time one of my children told me, "You're not like other parents," I wasn't sure if it was a compliment or a complaint.

It was both.

They meant: You push us. You expect more. You don't let us coast. You're always talking about our future, our goals, our potential.

But they also meant: You show up. You listen. You apologize when you're wrong. You're present even when you're busy.

That's intentional parenting. That's what breaking generational patterns looks like in action.

It's not about being perfect. It's about being purposeful. It's about recognizing that the way you were raised—both the good and the not-so-good—doesn't have to be the way you raise your children. You get to choose differently.

RHONA J. VEGA

WHAT DOES "BREAKING GENERATIONAL PATTERNS" REALLY MEAN?

Let's be clear about what we're talking about. Breaking generational patterns doesn't mean rejecting everything our parents taught us. Many of us were raised by people who did the best they could with what they had.

Breaking generational patterns means:

- Keeping what served us
- Releasing what harmed us
- Intentionally choosing how we show up as parents

It means recognizing that some parenting approaches worked in a different era, but don't serve our children today. It means understanding that our parents may have parented out of survival, but we have the opportunity to parent from a place of intention and healing.

Most importantly, it means that we're not repeating patterns unconsciously. We're making active, informed choices about how we raise our children.

The first example that comes to mind is parentification—making the oldest child a "third parent."

My oldest sibling, my sister, experienced this. I'm the baby and she is seventeen years older than me. Now at 60 and 77, I still hear the pain from my mom's decisions. My mom was basically tricked into moving to New York City by her then-husband.

She left her father, stepmother, and her entire supportive village in North Carolina by boarding a bus with four children—a preteen girl and three boys under six. There was no apartment as promised, and there was no money to return back to North Carolina. She was told she'd made her bed, and now needed to lie in it.

Mom went into survival mode, I'm sure, and my sister became the third parent. She talks often about raising our brothers and the chaos they caused, and Mom's extreme expectations of her as a young child. I feel like it made my sister's childhood hard.

This awareness shaped how I parented. I was determined not to put that burden on my oldest daughter. Yes, she helped with her siblings sometimes—that's family. But I never made her responsible for raising them. I never made her sacrifice her childhood to be a third parent. I hired help when I needed it, even when we couldn't afford it, because I saw what parentification did to others.

Did I get everything right? No. But I consciously chose not to repeat that pattern. And my daughter got to be a kid, even while being the oldest of five.

THE PATTERNS WORTH KEEPING

Before we talk about what to change, let's honor what our parents got right.

Many of us were raised to have:

- A strong work ethic
- Respect for elders
- An appreciation for the value of education
- Knowledge of the importance of family
- Faith and a spiritual foundation
- Resilience in the face of adversity

These aren't patterns to break. These are foundations to build on.

The question isn't, "Should I reject everything my parents taught me?" The question is, "How do I keep the good while releasing the harmful?"

SHIFTING FROM SURVIVAL PARENTING TO INTENTIONAL PARENTING

Many of our parents were in survival mode—doing whatever it took to keep us fed, safe, and alive in a world that wasn't built for us to thrive.

That kind of parenting made sense. It was necessary. But survival parenting often comes with:

- Emotional suppression ("Stop crying, or I'll give you something to cry about.")
- Authoritarian control ("Because I said so.")
- Limited explanation ("You don't need to know why, just do it.")
- Performance-based love ("You better bring home good grades.")

Our parents weren't wrong. They were doing what they knew how to do.

But we have the opportunity to shift from survival parenting to intentional parenting. We can parent from a place of:

- Emotional awareness and validation
- Healthy boundaries with age-appropriate autonomy
- Clear communication and explanation
- Unconditional love with high expectations

This isn't rejecting our parents. It's building on their foundation.

WHAT HEALTHY GENERATIONAL PARENTING LOOKS LIKE

Healthy generational parenting is about creating new patterns that serve our children while honoring what our parents taught us.

Here's what it looks like in practice:

High Expectations + High Support

- **Unhealthy pattern:** "You better get all A's or else."
- **Healthy pattern:** "I believe you're capable of excellence. What do you need from me to reach your goals?"

The difference? We're still setting high standards, but we're also providing the support to reach them.

Clear Communication

- **Unhealthy pattern:** "Because I said so. Don't question me."
- **Healthy pattern:** "Let me explain why this rule exists. I'm open to hearing your thoughts."

The difference? We maintain authority while valuing our child's voice.

Emotional Validation

- **Unhealthy pattern:** "Stop being so sensitive. You're fine."
- **Healthy pattern:** "I can see you're upset. Tell me what's going on."

The difference? We acknowledge feelings even when we can't change the situation.

Boundaries With Respect

- **Unhealthy pattern:** "My house, my rules. You have no say."
- **Healthy pattern:** "This is what's non-negotiable and why. On other things, let's discuss."

The difference? We're still the parent, but we respect our child as a person.

Accountability Over Shame

- **Unhealthy pattern:** "You're so irresponsible. You never do anything right."
- **Healthy pattern:** "That choice didn't work out. What will you do differently next time?"

The difference? We address the behavior, not the child's worth.

Connection Over Control

- **Unhealthy pattern:** Monitoring every move out of fear
- **Healthy pattern:** Building trust while maintaining appropriate oversight

The difference? The goal is having a healthy relationship, not just demanding compliance.

My title at work is "Success Coach." I felt fear when accepting the role, because it felt like a deep responsibility over someone's life! But I believe in the six-step plan above. It's what I do at home, and it's how I operate my businesses, Parent Matterz and Early Start Consulting. These are our core values—why I do this work. I help youth, including my own, discover their gifts and passions through exposure. I'm a huge fan of developing skill sets that will benefit them as they transition into adulthood.

Goal setting is key.

Let me share a specific example: I remember seeing my son light up when he took a coding class in fifth grade. That spark was undeniable. So I did research to find opportunities to continue his exposure in these areas.

He is the only one of my children who identified their passion so young and followed it all the way through their college major and career. Now he's a software engineer, and he thanks me for choosing to buy the swim club membership each year for the seven of us versus buying video game consoles that would have stunted his creativity and left him addicted to video gaming at age twenty-four.

But here's what made the difference: I didn't just expose him to opportunities. I helped him develop the skills to *capitalize* on them.

I often had to carve out time for each child. One hour on Saturdays to sit down (both with our computers) to apply to high schools, enrichment programs, scholarships, etc. We even practiced drafting professional emails. I highly recommend sending a year-end email or cards to all the folks who have poured into your children—teaching gratitude and relationship management.

Checking emails was a big hurdle with my sons. We created professional email accounts that I could also check for them because we saw many youth, including my own, miss opportunities because they weren't checking their emails regularly. My son actually missed free housing when he was interning at Meta his first year because he missed an email.

Helping students identify growth areas is important. I praised their greatness, but I also helped them learn to converse by getting to the point. That was a real class—how to communicate effectively. I taught them how to network by taking them to local galas and events and letting them watch me work a room.

This is what the Success Coach approach looks like in practice: Identify the passion, provide the exposure, develop the skills, create the systems, and stay involved—without micromanaging. It's intentional. It's consistent. And it works.

THE TRUST THAT HEALTHY PARENTING BUILDS

One of the most powerful testimonies to healthy generational parenting is the relationship it creates between parent and child.

Congresswoman Nikema Williams watched this unfold with my daughter at Spelman College. She observed: "I watched her grow into a young adult who genuinely wanted to spend time with her mother, and that spoke volumes. She knew she could come to Rhona with the good, the bad, and everything in between — that kind of trust doesn't happen by accident; it's built through consistency, love, and intentional parenting."

That's the goal. Not a child who blindly obeys out of fear. A child who trusts you enough to be honest with you. A child who wants to spend time with you. A child who comes to you with problems, not because they have to, but because they know you'll help.

That trust is built through:

- Showing up consistently
- Keeping your promises
- Apologizing when you're wrong
- Listening without judgment
- Respecting their feelings
- Following through on consequences fairly
- Celebrating who they are, not just what they achieve

HOW CHILDREN RESPOND TO INTENTIONAL PARENTING

When you parent with intention—when you break patterns you inherited that no longer serve your children and replace them with healthy ones—your children respond in powerful ways.

They become confident. One mentor who worked with my sons observed: "They were challenged at home to be great at all times… They were highly supported and encouraged to take risks and to go outside of their realm of comfort." That combination of high expectations and high support creates confidence, not fear.

They develop resilience. My son reflected on his upbringing: "As a Black man in a white world and not-so-diverse industry, you're gonna be faced with so many challenges. Getting set up in a position to succeed and perform well beyond 'their' benchmarks for you is something I will always be thankful for mom giving to me."

They appreciate the investment. My daughter said it clearly: "As I continued to grow, I was very grateful for the opportunities. I was able to explore several fields, go to a variety of programs while getting to meet new people."

They become self-aware. Even young children recognize healthy parenting. Kai, age twelve, said of his mother: "She shows us what good work ethics looks like…She always puts us first."

This is what healthy generational parenting produces: children who are confident, resilient, grateful, and self-aware.

PRACTICAL WAYS TO BREAK UNHEALTHY PATTERNS

Breaking patterns requires awareness and action. Here are concrete steps:

1. Identify what you want to change

Ask yourself: What did my parents do that I don't want to repeat? Be specific. "They yelled a lot" is a start. "They yelled when they were stressed, instead of explaining what they needed" is better.

2. Understand the why behind the pattern

Our parents weren't trying to hurt us. They were doing what they knew. Understanding the context doesn't excuse harm, but it helps us respond with compassion rather than bitterness.

3. Decide what you'll do instead

Don't just stop the unhealthy pattern. Replace it with a healthy one. If your parent criticized constantly, commit to affirming your child regularly. If your parent was emotionally distant, commit to emotional availability.

4. Communicate your intentions to your children

Let your kids know you're parenting differently on purpose. "I'm working on being more patient when I'm stressed. If I raise my voice, I'll apologize. I'm not perfect, but I'm trying."

5. Get support

Breaking generational patterns is hard work. Find a therapist, join a parenting group, connect with other parents who are on the same journey. You don't have to do this alone.

6. Give yourself grace

You will slip up. You'll hear your parent's voice come out of your mouth. You'll react in ways you swore you wouldn't. That's normal. What matters is that you recognize it, own it, and recommit to doing better.

In this exact moment, at 4:19 a.m., a few days before Thanksgiving, I'm sitting with the reality that I probably did a lot wrong.

Mental health therapy has been a norm in my house since my oldest was seven. Due to physical and emotional traumas we experienced in my relationships with their dads, I needed help. So for thirty years, I have been learning to love myself, accept and own my choices, and become more self-aware so I can model better behavior.

I definitely know I parented so much better with the last three kids because I was, for the first time since age nineteen, in a stable environment. Sixteen years of instability did a number on me, and I'm sure I did a number on my kids.

Here's what I've learned: Self-awareness is an ongoing journey, not a destination. I've definitely been told that I "threatened" my kids in a sense—" If you don't do it this way, then you will suffer consequences." Not harm from me, but long-term consequences. That came from a place of love and fear—I didn't want them to struggle the way I had struggled financially. I wanted them to have better career options and access to generational, wealth-building wages, not minimum wages.

But I've had to ask myself: Was that the healthiest approach? Was I parenting from trauma, or from intention?

The answer is probably both.

What I'm learning, even now, is that evolving our parenting legacy isn't about being perfect. It's about being willing to look at ourselves honestly, to admit when we've fallen short, and to keep growing. It's about giving ourselves grace while also committing to do better.

I'm still in therapy. I'm still learning. I'm still asking my adult children for feedback. And I'm still evolving. That's the work.

THE SUCCESS COACH APPROACH

One practical framework for healthy generational parenting is to see yourself as your child's success coach, not their drill sergeant.

A drill sergeant demands perfection through fear and control.

A success coach develops potential through support and guidance.

A drill sergeant says: "You better get straight A's."

A success coach says: "What are your goals this semester? How can I support you in reaching them?"

A drill sergeant says: "You're lazy and irresponsible."

A success coach says: "I notice you're struggling with time management. Let's create a system that works for you."

A drill sergeant punishes mistakes harshly.

A success coach uses mistakes as teaching moments.

HOW TO CREATE A SUCCESS COACH PLAN FOR YOUR CHILD:

Step 1: Identify Their Strengths

What is your child naturally good at? What do they love? Make sure they know you see their gifts.

Step 2: Identify Growth Areas Together

Don't impose your agenda. Ask your child: "What skills do you want to develop? What areas do you want to improve in?"

Step 3: Set Goals Collaboratively

Create goals together. When children have input, they're more invested in the outcome.

Step 4: Provide Support, Not Control

Your role is to remove barriers, provide resources, and offer accountability—not to micromanage every step.

Step 5: Celebrate Effort, Not Just Results

Did your child work hard, even if the outcome wasn't perfect? Celebrate that. You're teaching them that growth matters more than perfection.

Step 6: Adjust As Needed

Check in regularly. What's working? What's not? Be flexible.

WHEN YOU'RE DOING IT RIGHT, KIDS NOTICE

The beautiful thing about healthy generational parenting is that children recognize it—even if they don't always appreciate it in the moment.

The mentor who worked with my sons noted: "They were trained at home to understand you must be prepared at all times if you plan to succeed, and you can't use excuses as a crutch for why you fail. They were highly supported and encouraged to take risks."

That's not luck. That's intentional parenting paying off.

Your children are watching how you:

- Handle stress
- Treat others
- Apologize when wrong
- Follow through on promises
- Manage disappointment
- Celebrate success
- Respond to failure
- Practice self-care with breaks and resets

They're learning not just from what you say, but from what you do.

THE LONG-TERM OUTCOME

Breaking generational patterns isn't about immediate gratification. It's about long-term outcomes.

You're raising adults, not just children.

You're creating a family culture that your children will carry into their own parenting one day.

You're showing them that it's possible to honor where you come from while choosing something different for the future.

You're breaking cycles of harm while preserving values that matter.

That's legacy work. And it starts with the daily choice to parent with intention.

ACTION ITEMS FOR PARENTS

1. Identify One Pattern to Break

This week, choose one specific pattern from your upbringing that you want to do differently. Write it down. Be specific about what you'll do instead.

2. Have a Conversation About Parenting Intentions

Sit down with your child (when age-appropriate) and share: "I'm working on parenting differently than I was raised: [describe the specific pattern]. You might notice me doing [new behavior]. If I slip up, please know I'm trying."

3. Create a Success Coach Plan

Choose one area where your child wants to grow. Sit down together and create a plan using the six steps outlined above. Schedule your first discovery call with our team.

4. Practice Emotional Validation This Week

Every time your child expresses a difficult emotion this week, respond with validation first before trying to fix or minimize. "I can see you're really upset. Tell me more about what's happening."

5. Celebrate One Character Strength

Identify one character strength in your child that has nothing to do with achievement (kindness, courage, creativity, perseverance). Tell them specifically what you see and why you're proud.

6. Seek Support for Your Own Healing

If breaking generational patterns is bringing up pain from your own childhood, reach out for support. Find a therapist, join a support group, or connect with a trusted mentor.

SHARE THE MIC

"**I WATCHED MY INTERN GROW** into a young adult who genuinely wanted to spend time with her mother, and that spoke volumes. She knew she could come to Rhona with the good, the bad, and everything in between. That kind of trust doesn't happen by accident; it's built through consistency, love, and intentional parenting. Seeing their relationship up close showed me what it looks like to balance parenting and purpose. As a mom, I hope my son Carter and I continue building the same trust-filled, open bond that I witnessed between Rhona and her baby girl."

—*Congresswoman Nikema W.*

"They were challenged at home to be great at all times. They had sisters who were also high achievers, so they had big shoes to step into. They were trained at home to understand that you must be prepared at all times if you plan to succeed, and you can't use excuses as a crutch for why you fail.

They were highly supported and encouraged to take risks and to go outside of their realm of comfort. Her kids may not have always enjoyed the process, but they definitely reaped the benefits of the outcomes. They are each successful in their own professional paths and understand that they must give back (lift as you climb). They share the importance of acquiring the fundamental skills of connecting with people, mastering your craft, and continuing to learn and grow, personally and professionally."

—*Dale F., Parent, Executive, and Mentor*

"When I was younger, I thought my mom's work was so inspiring. She was aiming to do work to benefit students, highlighting a variety of opportunities to those from historically excluded communities. At times, I was frustrated that I was involved in a program when I wanted to be at home relaxing. However, as I continued to grow, I was very grateful for the opportunities.

I was able to explore several fields and go to a variety of programs while getting to meet new people. They were all enriching experiences, and I learned about different career fields and myself along the way. One thing I would say to other students and parents is that exploring different paths while you're young is so beneficial. It's good to try because you may never know what you will be interested in. And finding out that you don't like something is just as beneficial."

—*Janiene, Higher Ed Executive, Spelman and NYU Alum*

"She shows us what a good work ethic looks like, and I know she's working hard to provide for us. I appreciate everything she does for us. She always puts us first."

—*Kai M., Age Twelve, Seventh Grade*

Need support?
Book a Complimentary Discovery Call

https://calendly.com/parentmatterz/early-start
Consulting-Discovery-Call

CHAPTER FIVE
COLLEGE READINESS ISN'T JUST FOR RICH PRIVILEGED KIDS

College readiness shouldn't be reserved for families who can afford SAT tutors, college counselors, and campus tours across the country.

But too often, that's exactly what it feels like.

I've watched brilliant students—kids with drive, talent, and potential—miss out on opportunities simply because no one taught them how to navigate the system. They didn't know about fee waivers. They'd never visited a college campus. They had no idea what questions to ask, or how to advocate for themselves.

Meanwhile, wealthy students were being prepped with test prep courses, essay coaches, and strategic planning sessions that cost thousands of dollars—sometimes, all before they even began high school.

That gap? It's not about intelligence. It's about access.

And I'm here to tell you: You can close that gap. Your child can be college-ready without spending a fortune. You can level the playing field with knowledge, strategy, and hustle.

Let me show you how.

THE MYTH OF THE IVY LEAGUE PATH

Let's start by dismantling a dangerous myth: that Ivy League schools are the only path to success.

Don't get me wrong—if your child gets into Harvard, Yale, or Princeton, that's incredible. Celebrate it. But the idea that your child has to get into an Ivy League school to have a successful future? That's a lie that keeps too many families stressed, broke, and missing better opportunities.

Here's the truth: Fit matters more than prestige.

A student who thrives at a state school where they're getting hands-on experience, building relationships with professors, and graduating debt-free is better positioned than a student who's miserable at an Ivy League school, drowning in student loans, and struggling to keep up.

I've seen kids turn down full rides to state schools to attend prestigious universities where they graduated with $100,000 in debt and no job prospects. I've also seen kids attend "lesser-known" schools, excel, get incredible internships, and land well-paying jobs at top companies.

The name on the diploma matters less than what your child does while they're there.

So instead of obsessing over rankings and prestige, focus on these questions:

- Does this school offer strong programs in my child's area of interest?
- Will my child get individual attention and mentorship?

- What are the internship and career placement rates?
- Can my child graduate with minimal debt?
- Will my child be happy and supported here?

Those questions matter more than whether U.S. News ranks the school in the top twenty.

THE 800-STUDENT WORKSHOP THAT CHANGED EVERYTHING

I was invited to speak at the New Jersey statewide Equal Opportunity Fund (EOF) conference at Montclair State University. Eight hundred incoming, first-generation college students filled the auditorium—young people who were about to step into spaces their families had never navigated before.

The energy was electric.

Having my two older brothers there with me was magical. They weren't just there to support me—they were part of the message. Here we were: three siblings who came from the same neighborhood, the same circumstances, proving that college access isn't about perfection. It's about persistence.

I talked about what nobody tells first-generation students: You don't have to have it all figured out, asking for help isn't weakness, and your background is your strength, not your disadvantage. I talked about the hidden resources on campus they'd never think to look for. I talked about how to advocate for yourself when the system feels overwhelming.

The students were so engaged. They participated. They asked questions. They nodded in recognition when I named things they'd been feeling, but didn't have words for.

After my talk, dozens of students came up to me. They wanted selfies. They asked for my contact information. Some said, **"I didn't even know I needed this information."** Several scheduled discovery calls on the spot to keep the conversation going.

This event mattered because it reminded me of something I already knew but needed to see at scale: **Information is power.** And when you put the right information in front of students who are hungry for it, at the right time, in a way that makes them feel seen and capable—they run with it.

I can't wait to do this worldwide—encouraging students on small stages and large stages, one conversation at a time.

COLLEGE READINESS STARTS EARLY

Here's what most families don't realize: College readiness doesn't start senior year. It doesn't even start junior year. It starts in middle school. I'm not saying your seventh grader needs to be touring campuses, but I am saying touring campuses as early as kindergarten is a good idea…even if it's an event on the campus.

Here's what to focus on:

- Building good study habits
- Engaging with tutors and mentors
- Letting teachers know what kind of study skills you want your student to leave high school with. (Set the expectation with school professionals.)
- Getting involved in activities they care about
- Learning to advocate for themselves
- Understanding that grades matter
- Starting to think about their interests and strengths

By the time they hit high school, college readiness should be part of the conversation—not in a stressful, pressure-filled way, but in a "let's start planning for your future" way.

The college board has a great timeline for your reference. https://advancedcollegeplanning.net/the-complete-college-planning-timeline/

The earlier you start, the less stressful the process becomes.

THE FAFSA ISN'T OPTIONAL

If there's one thing I want every parent to understand, it's this: The FAFSA is not optional.

I don't care if you think you make too much money to qualify for aid. I don't care if you think the process is too complicated. I don't care if you're scared to share your financial information.

Fill. Out. The. FAFSA.

The Free Application for Federal Student Aid (FAFSA) is the gateway to federal grants, loans, and work-study programs. But it's also used by many colleges to determine institutional aid. If you don't fill it out, you're leaving money on the table—sometimes tens of thousands of dollars.

Here's what you need to know:

The FAFSA opens on October 1st every year. Don't wait until spring. File as soon as possible, because some aid is first-come, first-served.

You need your tax returns. Have your most recent tax return ready. If you haven't filed yet, use estimates and update later.

Your child needs an FSA ID. Both you and your child will need to create an FSA ID to sign the FAFSA electronically. Do this before you start the application.

It's free. Never pay anyone to fill out the FAFSA. The application is free, and there are free resources to help you complete it.

Mistakes can cost you. Double-check everything before submitting. Small errors can delay your aid or reduce the amount you receive.

You have to do it every year. FAFSA isn't a one-time thing. You'll need to complete it annually for as long as your child is in school.

QUESTIONS TO ASK ON EVERY COLLEGE VISIT

Campus visits are critical, but only if you're asking the right questions. Don't just walk around admiring the buildings and listening to the tour guide's memorized script. Dig deeper.

Here are the questions every parent and student should ask:

About academics:

- What's the average class size in my major?
- How accessible are professors outside of class?
- What percentage of classes are taught by graduate students vs. professors?
- What kind of academic support is available (tutoring, writing centers, etc.)?

About career preparation:

- What's the job placement rate for graduates in my major?
- Does the school have an internship or co-op program?
- What companies recruit on campus?
- Is there a career services office, and what do they offer?

About finances:

- What scholarships are available, and how do I apply?
- What's the average student loan debt for graduates?
- Are there work-study opportunities on campus?
- What happens to my financial aid if I don't maintain a certain GPA?

About student life:

- What support services are available (mental health, tutoring, mentoring)?
- What percentage of students live on campus vs. commute?
- How diverse is the student body?
- What's the graduation rate, and why do students leave?

Don't be afraid to ask hard questions. This is a major investment, and you deserve real answers.

THE COLLEGE VISIT THAT CHANGED THE DREAM

Vanessa reached out to Parent Matterz after seeing me and my son on an NBC special called *Being Black Behind The Wheel*. She was a high school student in Newark with a lifelong dream of studying business at Stanford University.

The NBC producers connected us, and I immediately enrolled her in the very first Junior Jump Start program. The information was life-changing for her.

When she told me her school didn't have the resources to support her Stanford dream, I immediately connected her to mentors who could pour into her. One of those mentors was Robyn, a force who had already helped my daughter achieve her dream of attending Spelman College. Robyn understood what it took to navigate elite college admissions, and she invested in Vanessa with the same care and expertise.

The results were stunning. Vanessa didn't just get accepted to Stanford—she got into several Ivy League schools and colleges of her choice. She also received a prestigious national scholarship that would cover full tuition to any school she attended.

Her parents were thrilled. Stanford had been the dream for years. They planned a family visit to campus.

But when Vanessa stepped onto Stanford's campus, something didn't feel right. She couldn't name it at first—the school was beautiful, prestigious, everything she thought she wanted. But something in her gut said, "This isn't it."

She was sad. Confused. She'd worked so hard for this dream, and now that it was within reach, it didn't feel like home.

So she visited Harvard.

And the moment she stepped on campus, she felt it. This was where she belonged.

That's the power of visiting colleges before you commit. You can research rankings and read brochures all day, but nothing replaces standing on campus, sitting in the student center, walking the paths, and asking yourself, "Can I see myself here?"

Vanessa trusted her gut. She chose Harvard. And now, as a thriving college senior, she looks back on that decision as one of the best she ever made.

Her parents are forever grateful—not because we got her into Stanford, but because we helped her find the tools, the mentors, and the confidence to choose the school that was right for *her*, not just the school that sounded impressive.

That's what college readiness really means. It's not just about getting in. It's about knowing what you need to thrive once you're there.

SCHOLARSHIPS ARE EVERYWHERE

One of the biggest myths about college is that scholarships are only for straight-A students with perfect test scores.

That's not true.

There are scholarships for:

- Students who are the first in their family to attend college
- Students from specific geographic areas
- Students pursuing specific majors
- Students with specific talents (art, music, athletics, leadership)
- Students who write compelling essays about their experiences
- Students with massive volunteer hours, who created an organization, who have had to relocate, or who have lost a parent

Your child doesn't have to be valedictorian to get scholarship money. They just have to be willing to apply.

Here's my advice:

- **Start searching early.** Sophomore or junior year is not too soon to start looking for scholarships.
- **Apply broadly.** Don't just go for the big, national scholarships. Apply to local ones too—they often have less competition. Many local organizations, Greek organizations, and alumni offer local scholarships.
- **Treat scholarship applications like a part-time job.** Set aside time every week to search and apply. The more you apply for, the better your chances.
- **Reuse essays when possible.** Be very mindful and remember to change the names of the college or scholarship when reusing essays. ALWAYS have several people read and edit your work

before submitting. Many scholarship applications ask similar questions. Write strong essays and adapt them for different applications.
- **Don't ignore small scholarships.** A $500 scholarship might not seem like much, but if you win five of them, that's $2,500. It adds up.
- **Watch deadlines closely.** Set reminders and submit early. Late applications won't be considered. Apply early, closer to the application opening. Many tech issues happen on deadline dates. Remember you want to stand out, so aim to be the first to apply.

THE SCHOLARSHIP WINNERS WHO MADE IT HAPPEN

I've watched so many students win significant scholarship money that it's hard to choose just one story. And honestly? That's a blessing to be able to say.

The amounts range from $10,000 per year to full tuition scholarships worth up to $70,000 annually. These students have gone on to attend Spelman, Howard, Harvard, Cornell, Muhlenberg, Long Island University, and so many other schools.

What made their applications stand out? A well-rounded, robust resume that included:

- College enrichment programs (like the ones we talked about earlier)
- College credit earned in high school
- Strong standardized test scores (this unlocks a lot of money)
- Solid GPA
- Professional development and exposure opportunities
- Leadership roles and consistent community service

Here's what I want you to understand: These components didn't happen by accident. These students built their resumes intentionally over four years because they knew what scholarship committees were looking for.

One student received a $20,000 scholarship in his senior year that allowed him to pay off any student loan debt he'd accumulated and use the remainder for off-campus housing. Another won a $10,000 scholarship from an application she found in the Parent Matterz newsletter—proof that opportunities are everywhere if you're paying attention.

The scholarships are real. The money is out there. Your job is to help your child build the resume that makes them competitive and to apply consistently. That's how you turn scholarship opportunities into actual dollars.

YOU DON'T HAVE TO DO THIS ALONE

One of the biggest barriers to college readiness is isolation. Parents feel like they're supposed to figure it all out on their own, and students feel like they're navigating a maze with no map.

But you don't have to do this alone.

Reach out to your child's guidance counselor. Yes, I know they're overworked and understaffed. But they have resources. Schedule a meeting. Ask questions. Stay on their radar.

Connect with other parents. Create a group chat with parents whose kids are in the same grade. Share information about college fairs, scholarship opportunities, and application deadlines.

Use free resources. College Board, Khan Academy, and FAFSA.gov all offer free tools and information. Take advantage of them.

Look for community programs. Many nonprofits, churches, and

community organizations offer free college prep workshops. Find them and show up.

Hire help if you can afford it. If you have the budget, a college counselor or essay coach can be worth the investment. But if you can't afford it, don't panic—there are free alternatives.

MAKING COLLEGE ACCESSIBLE FOR EVERY FAMILY

College readiness isn't about privilege. It's about preparation.

It's about knowing the system and working it to your advantage.

It's about starting early, asking questions, and refusing to let financial barriers keep your child from pursuing higher education.

Your child deserves a shot at college, and you have the power to make it happen—not by spending money you don't have, but by being strategic, informed, and relentless.

Let's make sure every child, regardless of their zip code or family income, has access to the education they deserve.

ACTION ITEMS FOR PARENTS

1. Start a College Savings Plan—Even If It's Small

Open a 529 plan or a dedicated savings account and contribute what you can—even if it's just $25 a month. Small, consistent contributions add up over time.

2. Create a College Planning Timeline

Sit down with your child and map out what needs to happen each year from now until graduation. Pin it somewhere visible and revisit it every semester.

3. Visit Four College Campuses Each Year, Starting in Middle School

It doesn't have to be a school your child is serious about—just visit one to start making college feel real and accessible. Ask the questions listed in this chapter.

4. Set Up Your FAFSA ID

Go to studentaid.gov and create FSA IDs for both you and your child. Do this now, before application season, so you're ready when the FAFSA opens.

5. Research Four Scholarships Each Month

Spend one hour this month searching for scholarships your child might be eligible for. Create a simple spreadsheet with deadlines, requirements, and links. The goal isn't to apply yet—it's to see what's out there and what qualifications they're looking for.

Here's why this matters: When you research scholarships early—starting in eighth or ninth grade—you learn what students need to qualify. Presidential scholarships? They require a certain GPA, leadership roles, and community service hours. Full-ride scholarships? Many require specific SAT/ACT scores and demonstrated financial need.

Once you know the requirements, you can work backward. Your child has four years to build the resume that matches the scholarship criteria. Start early, and by senior year, they'll have dozens of opportunities they're actually qualified for—not scrambling at the last minute, hoping something fits.

Build the habit of researching regularly. Make it routine. The scholarships are out there. You just have to know where to look and what they're asking for.

6. Schedule a Meeting with Your Child's Guidance Counselor

Do this each semester, beginning in middle school. You want to be top of mind when opportunities arise. Don't wait until senior year.

Schedule a meeting now to discuss your child's college plans, get advice, and ask about resources available through the school.

Go on organized tours of historically black colleges and universities (HBCUs) and other colleges. If there are none in your area, get your school to start one. That would count as leadership. You created an opportunity others can benefit from.

SHARE THE MIC

"**COLLEGE READINESS** started for me way before senior year. Every Saturday, my mom would sit down with each of us for an hour—one hour per kid—to work on applications, scholarships, and college prep. We'd draft professional emails to colleges and programs. We'd research scholarship opportunities and fill out applications.

She taught us how to write thank-you emails to mentors and program coordinators after opportunities. She created professional email accounts for us that she could monitor because she knew young people miss opportunities by not checking email regularly. At the time, I thought it was overkill. I wanted to be playing video games like other kids. But those Saturday sessions taught me discipline, time management, and how to advocate for myself in professional spaces.

When it came time to actually apply to colleges, I wasn't stressed. I knew how the process worked. I knew how to present myself. I knew how to follow up. That preparation didn't just get me into college—it set me up to excel once I got there. Now as a professional, I use those same skills: staying organized, following through on opportunities, maintaining professional communication. College readiness isn't just about getting accepted. It's about being prepared to succeed once you're there."

—*Seti V., Software Engineer,*
Howard School of Business Honors Alum

"When I was looking at colleges, I had options. I could have gone to schools with bigger name recognition or higher rankings on some list. But I chose Spelman College, and it was the best decision I ever made. I chose Spelman because I wanted to be in a space where I would be seen, supported, and surrounded by people who looked like me.

I wanted to attend an HBCU where Black women were centered, celebrated, and prepared for leadership. It wasn't about prestige—it was about fit. At Spelman, I wasn't just a number in a lecture hall. I built deep relationships with professors who knew my name and invested in my growth. I was mentored by incredible women, including now Congresswoman Nikema Williams, who saw my potential and pushed me to lead. I was surrounded by sisters who challenged me, supported me, and inspired me. That environment shaped who I am today.

What I wish I'd known during the application process is that the 'best' school isn't the one with the highest ranking—it's the one where you'll thrive. Where you'll be pushed and supported. Where you'll build a community that lasts long after graduation. Don't let anyone else define success for you. Find the place where you can be your full self and grow into the person you're meant to become."

—*Janiene T., Spelman College Alumna*

"Between the two of us, my brother and I received full tuition scholarships to our universities, plus additional outside scholarships that covered room and board. We're talking about graduating debt-free—completely.

How did we do it? We each applied for 50 or more scholarships. That's not a typo. Fifty. Or more.

Our strategy was simple but consistent: weekly applications during senior year and throughout college. We didn't stop once we got into school. We kept applying because scholarship opportunities don't end after freshman year.

Here's the key: We stored all our essays in Google Docs and carefully reused them, making sure we were still answering each specific question. Parent Matterz provided us with a scholarship tracker that was extremely helpful in keeping everything organized—deadlines, requirements, which essays worked for which scholarships.

What made our applications stand out? A combination of things: enrichment programs we'd participated in through Parent Matterz, our grades, consistent volunteer work, strong SAT scores, and the exposure we'd received through programs that helped us articulate our goals clearly.

How has graduating debt-free impacted our lives? Phenomenal. We're not starting our careers with $50,000, $100,000, or more in student loan debt. We can make career choices based on what we want to do, not what will pay off loans the fastest. We can start building generational wealth now instead of paying off the past.

Our advice to other students? Do everything Parent Matterz and this book suggest. Apply weekly. Track your deadlines. Reuse essays strategically. Don't stop after you get into college—keep applying. The money is out there, but you have to go get it. And trust me, it's worth it."

—*Parent Matterz, Scholarship Recipients*

Need support?
Book a Complimentary Discovery Call
https://calendly.com/parentmatterz/early-start Consulting-Discovery-Call

CHAPTER SIX
PRACTICAL DREAMING, CAREER EXPOSURE THAT WORKS

DREAMS WITHOUT STRATEGY ARE JUST WISHES.
I've watched too many young people dream about careers they know nothing about. They say they want to be lawyers because they saw it on TV. They want to be doctors because it sounds prestigious. They want to be entrepreneurs because they follow influencers who make it look easy.

But when you ask them, "What does a lawyer actually do all day?" or "What kind of doctor do you want to be?" or "What business problem are you trying to solve?"—they have no idea.

That's the difference between dreaming and practical dreaming.

Practical dreaming is when you take a vague aspiration and turn it into a concrete plan. It's when you bridge the gap between "I think I might like that" and "I know exactly what that career requires, and here's my path to get there."

This chapter is about helping your child move from fantasy to strategy—from dreaming about careers to actually preparing for them.

THE STUDENT WHO ALMOST QUIT—THEN THRIVED

"I wasn't a strong student. Most of my siblings were in advanced math classes in middle school, and I wasn't. I definitely struggled with self-confidence outside of sports and music. I had no clue about my future.

My mom scheduled a meeting with my middle school principal, and he strongly suggested I take only honors classes—and eventually AP classes in high school. I thought, *No way.* But my mom and my principal didn't accept that. He said, 'The worst thing that could happen is you drop back to regular classes if you really can't handle it.'

Not only did I survive high school—I thrived. I learned about skills and interests I never knew I had.

My mom connected me to my high school's support services for tutoring, counseling, and just a place to chill when I felt overwhelmed. They were a lifesaver. I tried to quit high school a few times. I even changed two of my classes because the fit wasn't right—even though those same teachers were my older sister's favorites. That was an eye-opener for my parents: Every kid is different. Like careers and colleges, you want to make sure it's a good fit.

My high school guidance counselor became a family friend and mentor after he began working in a different school district. He coached me through life, college, and career situations. He was one of my mom's go-to people when she needed us to take action.

Attending several pre-college programs—one to four weeks each, five total—was life-changing. It opened up my world. I was extremely pissed at my mom for making this a requirement to live in her house (the threat was we could go live with Grandma if we didn't want to follow her rules!). But meeting mentors, CEOs who looked like me doing big things, winning awards, traveling—it made me realize how small my world had been.

In high school, I got exposed to theater and ended up starring in a play, which helped me build confidence. That confidence eventually helped me create a successful YouTube channel, TejidotCom.

I used my newfound networking skills to gain access to internships. One summer program led to a full-tuition scholarship. I studied abroad, played music with a jazz band in Europe, and landed a prestigious job in finance after graduation.

Now I'm living a life I never dreamed of. I run a business outside of work and help my parents financially. All because my mom refused to let me think small."

—*Teji V., Finance Professional & Content Creator*

WHY "FOLLOW YOUR PASSION" ISN'T ENOUGH

We tell kids to follow their passion. But here's the problem: Most kids don't know what they're passionate about yet. And even if they do, passion alone doesn't pay bills.

I'm not anti-passion. I'm pro-strategy.

Passion is important, but it's not the whole equation. You also need:

- Skills that employers value
- Knowledge of how industries actually work
- A network of people who can open doors

- A realistic understanding of what the day-to-day work looks like

When we only focus on passion, we set kids up for disappointment. They chase dreams without understanding the work required to achieve them. They major in fields with no clear career path. They graduate with debt and no plan.

Practical dreaming is different. It says: "What are you curious about? Great. Now let's figure out what that career actually looks like, what skills you need, and how to get there."

It's not about crushing dreams. It's about making dreams achievable.

THE CAREER EXPOSURE GAP

Here's what happens when kids don't get career exposure:

They choose careers based on what they see around them. If all they know are teachers, nurses, retail workers, and police officers, those are the only careers they'll consider—not because they're passionate about them, but because they're the only options they know exist.

They make major life decisions (like choosing a college major) without understanding what jobs are available in that field or what those jobs pay.

They miss opportunities because they don't know what questions to ask or how to position themselves for internships, mentorships, or entry-level roles.

They graduate unprepared for the professional world because no one taught them how to network, interview, or navigate workplace culture.

The career exposure gap is real. And it disproportionately affects

Black and Brown students, first-generation college students, and kids from low-income families.

These students are just as smart and capable as their peers with more access. But their peers have been getting career exposure since middle school—shadowing parents at work, attending industry conferences, interning at family friends' companies, getting mentored by professionals in their networks.

If we want to level the playing field, we have to close the career exposure gap.

STARTING WITH WHAT THEY'RE CURIOUS ABOUT

Career exposure doesn't start with picking a job. It starts with noticing what your child is curious about.

Do they love building things? Do they ask a million questions about how stuff works? Do they light up when they're solving problems? Do they thrive when they're organizing people or events?

Those are clues.

Your job isn't to force them into a career. Your job is to help them explore their curiosity and see where it leads.

Here's how:

Ask open-ended questions. Instead of, "What do you want to be when you grow up?" try, "What kind of problems do you like solving?" or "When do you feel most excited about what you're doing?"

Notice what they're drawn to. Do they spend hours on YouTube learning about cars? Do they love creating TikToks? Do they ask about how buildings are designed? Follow those threads.

Connect their interests to careers they might not know exist. If they love video games, introduce them to game designers, animators, or software engineers. If they love fashion, show them careers in merchandising, textile design, or fashion marketing.

Expose them to multiple pathways. A kid who loves science doesn't have to be a doctor. They could be a lab technician, a pharmacist, a public health researcher, an environmental scientist, or a forensic analyst. Show them options.

The goal isn't to lock them into a career at age fourteen. The goal is to expand their sense of what's possible.

FROM EXPLORATION TO EXPERIENCE

Once your child has identified a field they're curious about, the next step is to help them experience it.

This is where practical dreaming becomes real.

Here's how to move from exploration to experience:

JOB SHADOWING

Reach out to professionals in your network (or your extended network) and ask if your child can shadow them for a day. Most professionals are honored to be asked and happy to share what they do.

What to ask: "My child is interested in [field]. Would it be possible for them to shadow you for a few hours to see what a day in your life looks like?"

INFORMATIONAL INTERVIEWS

Have your child interview professionals about their careers. This teaches them how to ask good questions, build relationships, and gather information.

Sample questions:

- What does a typical day look like for you?
- What do you love most about your job?
- What's harder than people think?
- What education or training did you need?
- What advice would you give someone interested in this field?

INTERNSHIPS AND SUMMER PROGRAMS

Look for internships, summer programs, and mentorship opportunities in fields your child is interested in. Many are free or low-cost.

Where to look:

- Local nonprofits and community organizations
- Colleges and universities (many offer high school programs)
- Professional associations (many have youth programs)
- Your employer (some companies offer "bring your child to work" programs or youth internships)

VOLUNTEER WORK

If formal internships aren't available, encourage your child to volunteer in a field they're curious about. Volunteering builds skills, creates connections, and gives them real-world experience.

Examples:

- A child interested in healthcare can volunteer at a hospital or nursing home.
- A child interested in law can volunteer at a legal aid clinic.

- A child interested in business can help a local small business with social media or marketing.

THE POWER OF "I TRIED IT AND DIDN'T LIKE IT"

Here's something we don't talk about enough: It's okay if your child tries something and realizes they don't like it.

In fact, that's valuable.

Figuring out what you don't want to do is just as important as figuring out what you do want to do.

I've seen students shadow a lawyer and realize they hate sitting at a desk all day. I've seen students volunteer at a hospital and realize they can't handle the sight of blood. I've seen students intern at a nonprofit and realize they thrive in fast-paced, for-profit environments.

That's not failure. That's clarity.

When your child tries something and says, "This isn't for me," celebrate that. They just saved themselves years of pursuing a path that wouldn't have made them happy.

Encourage them to cross things off the list. The goal isn't to find the perfect career at age sixteen. The goal is to gather data about what they enjoy, what they're good at, and what kind of work environment suits them.

BUILDING PRACTICAL SKILLS ALONGSIDE PASSION

Here's the truth: Even if your child doesn't know what they want to do yet, there are skills they can build now that will serve them in any career.

These are the skills that employers value across industries:

- **Communication:** Can they speak clearly? Write professionally? Present ideas confidently?
- **Critical thinking:** Can they analyze problems and come up with solutions?
- **Time management:** Can they meet deadlines and manage multiple priorities?
- **Collaboration:** Can they work well with others, even people they don't love?
- **Digital literacy:** Are they comfortable with technology, basic software, and online tools?
- **Professionalism:** Do they understand workplace norms like showing up on time, dressing appropriately, and taking feedback well?

These aren't sexy skills. Nobody dreams of being "really good at email." But these are the skills that get you hired, promoted, and respected.

Start building them now:

- Have your child email a professional to request an informational interview (teach them professional email etiquette).
- Ask them to research a career and present what they learned to the family.
- Encourage them to get a part-time job or volunteer position where they have to show up on time and work with others.
- Teach them how to shake hands, make eye contact, and introduce themselves confidently.

THE CAREER COLLAGE ACTIVITY

One of my favorite activities to do with young people is the Career Collage. It's simple, visual, and gets them thinking about their future in a creative way.

Here's how it works:

Step 1: Gather materials. You'll need magazines, scissors, glue, and poster board.

Step 2: Set the intention. Tell your child: "We're going to create a collage that represents what you want your life to look like in ten years. Don't overthink it—just cut out images and words that resonate with you."

Step 3: Cut and paste. Spend 30 to 60 minutes cutting out images, words, and phrases that represent:

- Careers they're curious about
- Lifestyles they want (travel, family, community involvement, etc.)
- Values that matter to them (creativity, helping others, financial security, etc.)
- Skills they want to build

Step 4: Discuss. When the collage is done, talk about what they chose. Ask:

- What patterns do you notice?
- What surprises you about what you picked?
- What careers might align with these interests and values?

This activity helps kids visualize their future in a concrete way. And it gives you insight into what matters to them.

CONNECTING TO REAL OPPORTUNITIES

Once your child has a clearer sense of what they're interested in, your job is to connect them to real opportunities.

This is where your network comes in.

You don't need to know CEOs or celebrities. You just need to know people—and be willing to ask.

How to connect your child to professionals:

Start with your inner circle. Who do you know personally who works in a field your child is interested in? Reach out.

Expand to your extended network. Post on social media: "My child is interested in [field]. Does anyone know someone who would be willing to chat with them for fifteen minutes?"

Use LinkedIn. Search for professionals in your area who work in fields your child is curious about. Send a polite message explaining your child's interest and asking if they'd be open to a brief conversation.

Attend industry events. Many professional associations host networking events, career fairs, or panels. Bring your child.

Leverage community organizations. Churches, youth programs, and nonprofits often have connections to professionals willing to mentor young people.

The ask doesn't have to be big. You're not asking for a job. You're asking for fifteen minutes of someone's time to answer questions or let your child shadow them for a few hours.

Most people will say yes. And if they say no, move on to the next person.

RHONA J. VEGA

Connecting Students to Career Opportunities: The Video Shadowing Experience

My youngest was a theater major in high school, but she wasn't sure if she preferred being in front of the camera or behind it. She needed exposure to help her figure it out.

An opportunity presented itself through my network: A well-known studio production company in NYC was offering high school students and young adults the chance to shadow professionals in various roles—operations management, lighting, graphics, audio, producing, robotics, and more.

I immediately connected my daughter and several other students to this once-in-a-lifetime opportunity. Over the course of two weeks, those students rotated through different departments, shadowing professionals in real production environments. One day, they'd shadow the technical director. The next day, they'd work with the graphics team or sit in on a production session. Some students shadowed in audio engineering. Others explored robotics and lighting design.

My daughter got to see every side of production—the creative work, the technical work, the behind-the-scenes coordination that makes a show come together. She shadowed producers, graphic designers, and operations managers. She asked questions. She observed professionals under pressure. She saw what it actually takes to work in media and entertainment.

As a result, she ended up studying communications and theater in college, and received an incredible scholarship. But more than that, the exposure was priceless. She got to eliminate career paths that didn't fit and confirm the ones that did—all before making a college decision.

Here's the beautiful part: I ran into the creator of that shadowing program this summer. God put us on the same ferry to Martha's Vineyard. It's been three years since that program. She's changed companies and careers since then, but she just won an Emmy for producing the Super Bowl halftime show.

That's the power of connection. You never know where one opportunity will lead—not just for the students, but for everyone involved.

WHEN YOUR CHILD HAS NO IDEA WHAT THEY WANT

What if your child has no idea what they're interested in? What if they shrug every time you ask about their future?

That's okay. Not every kid is a visionary at age fifteen.

Here's what to do:

- Expose them to everything. Take them to career fairs, industry panels, college campuses, workplaces. Let them see a wide range of options.
- Focus on skills, not careers. Even if they don't know what they want to do, they can still build communication skills, work ethic, and professionalism.
- Let them try lots of things. Encourage part-time jobs, volunteer work, and extracurriculars. Each experience teaches them something about themselves.
- Be patient. Some kids don't figure out their path until college—or even after. Your job is to keep exposing them to opportunities so that when clarity comes, they're prepared to act on it.

THE BELIEF NETWORK

One of the most powerful things you can give your child is what I call a Belief Network—a group of people who believe in them and their potential.

This includes:

- Family members who encourage them
- Teachers who see their strengths
- Mentors who invest in their growth
- Peers who push them to be better
- Professionals who open doors for them

When a child has a Belief Network, they don't just dream—they execute. Because they have people holding them accountable, cheering them on, and reminding them of what's possible.

Your job as a parent is to help build that network. Introduce your child to people who will pour into them. Create opportunities for them to be around excellence. Surround them with people who expect greatness from them.

A Belief Network doesn't just help your child get a job. It shapes how they see themselves and what they believe they're capable of.

MAKING CAREER EXPOSURE A LIFESTYLE

Career exposure isn't a one-time event. It's a lifestyle.

It's the conversations you have at the dinner table about work and careers. It's the professionals you bring into your child's life. It's the way you frame challenges as opportunities to build skills.

Make career exposure part of your family culture:

- Talk about your own career—what you love, what's hard, what you're learning.
- Point out careers in everyday life (the architect who designed a building, the engineer who created a product, the entrepreneur who started a business).

- Celebrate your child's curiosity and effort, not just outcomes.

Encourage them to try things, fail, learn, and try again. When career exposure becomes a lifestyle, your child doesn't just stumble into a career—they build one intentionally.

ACTION ITEMS FOR PARENTS

1. Create a Career Collage With Your Child

Set aside an evening to do this activity together. Use magazines, printouts, or digital tools to create a visual representation of what your child wants their life to look like in 10 years. Discuss what patterns emerge.

2. Identify Three Professionals Your Child Can Connect With

Think about people in your network (or people one connection away) who work in fields your child is curious about. Reach out this week and ask if they'd be willing to have a 15-minute conversation with your child.

3. Schedule a Job Shadowing or Informational Interview

Pick one professional from your list and set up a time for your child to shadow them for a few hours or interview them about their career. Prepare your child with questions to ask.

4. Encourage Your Child to Try Something New This Month

Sign them up for a volunteer opportunity, part-time job, or extracurricular activity related to a field they're curious about. Even if they end up not liking it, it's valuable information.

5. Start Building Their Belief Network

Write down the names of five to 10 people who believe in your child and could support them in different ways (mentors, teachers, family friends, professionals). Reach out to one person this week to deepen that connection.

6. Have a Career Conversation Over Dinner

Ask your child: "What kind of problems do you like solving?" or "When do you feel most excited about what you're doing?" Listen without judgment and follow their curiosity.

SHARE THE MIC

"**MY MOM** exposed me to technology and coding when I was in fifth grade through a coding class. I was the only kid in our family who identified a passion at a young age and followed it all the way through to a career. Looking back, those Saturday morning sessions where she sat with each of us for an hour to apply to programs, draft professional emails, and research opportunities—that was career exposure.

She taught us how to network by taking us to galas and showing us how to work a room. She created professional email accounts for us that she monitored because she knew youth miss opportunities by not checking their email. All of that practical skill-building prepared me for the professional world. Now, as a software engineer, I use those skills every single day—networking, professional communication, following through on opportunities. That early career exposure didn't just show me what was possible; it gave me the tools to actually get there."

—*Seti V., Software Engineer,*
Howard School of Business Honors Program alum

"Working with Rhona's children as their college counselor showed me the power of early, intentional career exposure. These weren't students stumbling into college decisions at the last minute. They'd been systematically exposed to different fields, taught how to research careers, and given the tools to articulate their interests and goals.

What stood out was their maturity in understanding that career exploration is a process—you try things, you learn what you like and don't like, and you adjust. That mindset doesn't happen by accident. It's the result of parents who create consistent opportunities for their children to explore, question, and discover. Career exposure matters because it transforms 'I don't know what I want to do' into 'Here are three paths I'm considering, and here's my plan to explore each one."

—*Dr. Frank A., College Coach*

"I attended a week-long summer enrichment program hosted by the National Association of Black Accountants in high school. Afterward, I told my mom I was not interested in accounting at all.

She congratulated me. She said, 'It's awesome to know what you don't like.'

I was still exploring because I honestly didn't know what I wanted to do.

A few years later, after another summer business leadership bootcamp, the program offered me full tuition if I attended their college. It was October of my senior year, and I already had a college and a scholarship lined up. I took the easy road and accepted, still not knowing what I wanted to study.

When we visited the campus again, my mom noticed they had a baseball team and a music studio—two of my passions. That sealed the deal.

I was accepted into a pilot program where former Wall Street executives groomed 40 scholars for high-paying corporate jobs.

Most professors came straight from the workforce, and the program included internship opportunities, networking events, travel, and intensive professional development.

Even though I didn't want to attend that week-long program in high school, I made a great impression on the professors. They remembered me and offered me a spot in the pilot program.

I thought I'd focus on marketing. Instead, I graduated with honors and landed an international tax consulting position with one of the top four accounting firms. Yes, accounting. The field I said I wasn't interested in.

Here's what I learned: The most valuable thing I gained from all those programs wasn't just knowing what careers existed—it was learning how to navigate professional spaces. I learned how to introduce myself confidently, ask good questions in informational interviews, follow up with thank-you notes, and present myself professionally. Those aren't skills you're born with. They're skills you build through practice.

When I got to college and later entered the professional world, I wasn't intimidated by networking events or office environments because I'd been in those spaces before. I knew the unwritten rules.

My advice to students? Stay open to everything and every opportunity. Listen to your parents and your village, who believe in you. Don't dismiss something just because it doesn't excite you at first—you might be surprised.

My advice to parents? Don't take no for an answer. Make them try it anyway. Even if they say they're not interested, the exposure matters. You never know what will stick.

And here's the thing: Don't just explore different careers—practice the skills you'll need in any career. Learn to communicate clearly, manage your time, work with people you don't necessarily like, and advocate for yourself. Those practical skills will serve you no matter what path you choose."

—*Long Island University Dean Scholar, Finance Manager*

Need support?
Book a Complimentary Discovery Call

https://calendly.com/parentmatterz/early-start
Consulting-Discovery-Call

CHAPTER SEVEN
THE BLUEPRINT FOR BIPOC YOUTH EMPOWERMENT

BIPOC—BLACK, INDIGENOUS, AND PEOPLE OF COLOR—IS A term that acknowledges the unique experiences and systemic barriers faced by communities of color in America. BIPOC youth don't just need exposure. They need systems that are built for them, by people who understand them.

For too long, youth empowerment programs have been designed by people who don't look like our kids, don't live in our communities, and don't understand the specific barriers our children face. The result? Programs that sound good on paper, but fail in practice. Programs that expect parents to navigate systems they were never taught to navigate. Programs that claim to serve "all youth," but center the experiences of white, middle-class families.

BIPOC youth need something different. They need programs that are culturally grounded, community-driven, and unapologetically designed to address the systemic barriers that hold them back.

This chapter is about building that blueprint—creating replicable systems that actually work for Black, Latino, Indigenous, and other youth of color.

THE BIPOC SUPERINTENDENT WHO OPENED THE DOOR

So many people come to mind when I think about the community leaders who helped me scale my impact. But one stands out: the new superintendent of our local public schools, who took a chance on me and allowed Parent Matterz to host the first-ever Youth Opportunity Expo.

Here's how it started. I attended a similar expo at my daughter's magnet high school—a school that wasn't very diverse. The event was exactly what you'd expect: not geared toward the BIPOC population. Many of the programs featured were super expensive, not very diverse, and not inclusive. As a parent, I knew that many families like mine are wary when their child might be "the One and Only" at an overnight or summer program. They'll likely have challenges fitting in and won't get the full experience.

God placed a dream on my heart: Create a similar expo, but open to all students—especially the ones who get overlooked.

I thought it was a brilliant idea to reach more youth. Until that point, I was reaching families one at a time. But this would allow 1,200 students an opportunity to experience all the resources, enrichment programs, mentorship opportunities, and local programs people overlook in their communities because they're busy working and commuting.

The superintendent said yes.

Five years later, another superintendent, Dr. Marnie Hazleton, said yes, and to date we have hosted two youth empowerment expos in her district, empowering thousands of students, including speed networking events as well.

We brought in 60 exhibitors—including local government, colleges, Greek life organizations, and community programs. We built in prizes and created a unique system to make sure students engaged one-on-one with representatives at multiple tables. We didn't just want them to walk through and grab flyers. We wanted them to ask questions, make connections, and leave with next steps.

That first expo was a game changer. It gave me the confidence to connect with other superintendents and school administrators in neighboring districts.

We've now hosted multiple expos, including two this year at the same high school. Each time, we add a twist to keep students engaged and ensure they're not just passing through—they're connecting.

That's what happens when a leader in power opens the door. One yes from the right person can reach 1,200 students at once. That's scale. That's impact. That's what BIPOC youth deserve.

WHY BIPOC YOUTH NEED TARGETED SUPPORT

Let me be clear: BIPOC youth are not broken. They are not deficient. They are not less capable than their white peers. But they are navigating systems that were not designed with them in mind.

They're dealing with:

- Under-resourced schools in their communities
- Colleges that don't recruit from their high schools
- Employers who overlook their resumes because of their names or zip codes

- Financial aid systems that penalize their families for not knowing how to navigate bureaucracy
- Networks that exclude them because they don't have the "right" connections

This isn't about individual failure. This is about systemic barriers. And if we want to empower BIPOC youth, we have to address those barriers head-on—not with generic programs that ignore race, but with targeted support that acknowledges the specific challenges our kids face.

Targeted support isn't unfair. It's equity.

When you build a wheelchair ramp, you're not giving wheelchair users an unfair advantage. You're leveling the playing field so they can access the same building everyone else can access.

That's what BIPOC-focused youth empowerment does. It levels the playing field.

WHAT MAKES BIPOC YOUTH EMPOWERMENT DIFFERENT

BIPOC youth empowerment isn't just exposure. It's exposure plus:

- Cultural affirmation
- Mentorship from people who look like them
- Support for navigating systems designed to exclude them
- Community accountability
- A focus on both individual success and collective liberation

Let me break that down.

CULTURAL AFFIRMATION

BIPOC youth grow up in a world that tells them they're not enough. Their hair is "unprofessional." Their names are "hard to pronounce." Their neighborhoods are "dangerous." Their cultures are "other."

Empowerment programs need to counter those messages by affirming who they are—not asking them to assimilate.

That means:

- Celebrating their cultures, languages, and identities
- Highlighting successful professionals who share their backgrounds
- Creating spaces where they see themselves reflected in leadership
- Teaching them that they don't have to code-switch or shrink themselves to succeed

MENTORSHIP FROM PEOPLE WHO LOOK LIKE THEM

Representation matters. When BIPOC youth see professionals who look like them, it changes what they believe is possible.

But it's not just about seeing someone who looks like you. It's about having access to someone who understands your lived experience—someone who knows what it's like to navigate predominantly white spaces, someone who can teach you how to advocate for yourself, someone who can validate the things you're experiencing.

BIPOC mentors provide something white mentors can't: lived experience with the same systems of oppression.

NAVIGATIONAL SUPPORT

College applications, financial aid, internships, scholarships, professional networks—these systems are complicated. And they're designed in ways that assume you have insider knowledge.

BIPOC families often don't have that insider knowledge, because they've been systematically excluded from these systems for generations.

Youth empowerment programs need to provide explicit navigational support:

- Walk them through the FAFSA step-by-step.
- Teach them how to write professional emails.
- Show them how to network, even when they don't have family connections.
- Help them understand unwritten rules about internships, interviews, and workplace culture.

Don't assume they already know. Teach them explicitly.

COMMUNITY ACCOUNTABILITY

BIPOC youth empowerment isn't just about individual success. It's about collective liberation.

That means teaching young people that their success is connected to their community's success. That they have a responsibility to lift as they climb. That their education, their career, and their platform are tools they can use to create change.

Community accountability keeps young people grounded. It reminds them where they came from and who they're responsible to.

BUILDING A REPLICABLE SUPPORT SYSTEM

If you want to empower BIPOC youth at scale, you can't do it alone. You need a system that other people can replicate.

Here's the blueprint:

Step 1: Start With Your Community

Don't start with a program. Start with relationships.

Who are the trusted adults in your community? Pastors, coaches, teachers, barbershop owners, business owners, elders?

Those are the people you need to partner with. Because BIPOC families trust people, not programs. Your job is to build relationships with those trusted adults and ask: "What do the young people in this community need? How can we work together to provide it?"

Step 2: Define Your Focus

You can't be everything to everyone. Pick a focus area and go deep.

Are you focused on:

- College readiness?
- Career exposure?
- Leadership development?
- Academic support?
- Mental health and wellness?
- Entrepreneurship?

Pick one or two areas and build your program around that. Trying to do everything dilutes your impact.

Step 3: Create a Cohort Model

Cohorts are powerful because they build community. When young people go through a program together, they hold each other accountable, support each other, and create lifelong networks.

Here's how to structure a cohort:

- Recruit 10–25 young people (small enough to build relationships, big enough to create peer momentum)
- Meet regularly (weekly or bi-weekly)
- Create a curriculum with clear goals and outcomes
- Build in mentorship, workshops, field trips, and hands-on experiences
- Celebrate milestones together

Cohorts also make your program replicable. Once you've run one cohort successfully, you can train someone else to run another cohort using the same model.

Step 4: Leverage Partnerships

You don't have to build everything from scratch. Partner with organizations that already have infrastructure, funding, or expertise.

Who can you partner with?

- Local colleges and universities (they often have programs for high school students)
- Nonprofits focused on youth development
- Businesses that want to invest in the community
- Faith-based organizations with space and networks
- Professional associations (many have youth chapters or mentorship programs)

Partnerships expand your reach without draining your capacity.

Step 5: Train Community Members to Lead

If you want your program to scale, you need to train other people to run it.

Identify community members who are passionate about youth empowerment, and teach them how to facilitate your program.

Provide them with:

- A clear curriculum and timeline
- Training on facilitation and mentorship
- Ongoing support and check-ins
- Access to resources (materials, speakers, funding)

When you train community members to lead, you multiply your impact. One program becomes five programs. Five programs become twenty.

Step 6: Measure and Iterate

How do you know if your program is working? You measure outcomes.

Track:

- How many young people participated?
- Did they complete the program?
- What skills did they gain?
- What opportunities did they access (internships, college admissions, scholarships)?
- What do they say about their experience?

Use that data to improve your program. What's working? What's not? What do young people say they need more of?

Don't just collect data for funders. Use it to make your program better.

STARTING SMALL: THE POWER OF A MICRO-GROUP

You don't need a $500,000 budget or a staff of twenty to empower BIPOC youth. You can start with a micro-group: just five to ten young people who meet regularly for a shared purpose.

Here are examples of micro-groups you could start:

- A college application support group for seniors
- A career exploration group for juniors
- A leadership development group for middle schoolers
- A scholarship application group
- A book club focused on BIPOC authors and themes

Micro-groups are powerful because:

- They're low-cost (you can meet in someone's living room, a library, or a church basement).
- They're flexible (you can meet weekly, monthly, or whenever works).
- They create accountability (when it's a small group, young people show up).
- They build deep relationships (small groups allow for meaningful connection).

I've seen micro-groups change lives. Don't underestimate what you can do with five committed young people and a few hours a month.

THE ROLE OF PARENTS IN YOUTH EMPOWERMENT

Parents are the most powerful advocates for their children. But many parents don't realize how much power they have.

Your role as a parent in youth empowerment isn't just to sign your child up for programs. Your role is to:

- Advocate for your child's needs in school, programs, and professional spaces.
- Connect your child to mentors and opportunities.
- Teach your child how to navigate systems that weren't built for them.
- Model what it looks like to advocate for yourself.
- Hold programs accountable (if they're not serving your child well, speak up).

You are not just a passive participant in your child's empowerment. You are a co-creator.

WHEN SYSTEMS FAIL, BUILD YOUR OWN

Sometimes the systems that are supposed to serve BIPOC youth fail. The schools may not care. The programs don't show up. The resources aren't there.

When that happens, you have two choices: wait for someone else to fix it, or build your own.

I've seen parents, educators, and community leaders build their own:

- Tutoring programs, when schools failed their kids
- Mentorship networks, when professional pipelines excluded them

- Scholarship funds, when financial aid wasn't enough
- College prep workshops, when guidance counselors were overwhelmed

You don't need permission to empower your community. You just need commitment.

WHAT BIPOC YOUTH DESERVE

BIPOC youth deserve more than survival. They deserve to thrive.

They deserve to see themselves reflected in leadership, in curricula, in mentorship, and in opportunity.

They deserve programs that don't just prepare them to fit into existing systems, but empower them to change those systems.

They deserve communities that invest in them, believe in them, and hold them accountable to their greatness.

This is the blueprint. Now it's time to build.

ACTION ITEMS FOR PARENTS AND COMMUNITY LEADERS

―――――――――――

1. Identify Three Trusted Adults in Your Community

Write down the names of three people in your community who young people trust and respect (coaches, teachers, pastors, business owners). Reach out to one of them this week to start a conversation about youth empowerment.

2. Start a Micro-Group

Gather five to 10 young people and commit to meeting once a month for six months. Pick a focus (college apps, career exploration, leadership development) and create a simple plan for what you'll do together. Schedule a strategy call with our coaches to help guide you.

3. Attend a Community Event

Go to a school board meeting, a town hall, a youth program showcase, or a community gathering. Show up and start building relationships with people already doing this work.

4. Complete the Partnership-Building Worksheet

Use the worksheet at the end of this chapter to identify potential partners in your area—organizations, businesses, or individuals who could support youth empowerment efforts.

5. Advocate for Your Child This Week

Identify one system or space where your child needs support (school, extracurricular program, workplace). Reach out to advocate for what they need. Model advocacy for your child.

6. Share Your Story

If you've benefited from a youth empowerment program, a mentor, or a community leader who invested in you, share that story with a young person. Let them know that the investment in them is part of a legacy.

PARTNERSHIP-BUILDING WORKSHEET

USE THIS WORKSHEET to identify potential partners for youth empowerment efforts in your community.

LOCAL ORGANIZATIONS

List five local nonprofits, faith-based organizations, or community groups that work with youth:

1. _____
2. _____
3. _____
4. _____
5. _____

EDUCATIONAL INSTITUTIONS

List three schools, colleges, or universities that might partner with you:

1. _____
2. _____
3. _____

BUSINESSES

List five local businesses or corporations that might provide funding, space, or mentorship:

1. _____
2. _____
3. _____
4. _____
5. _____

PROFESSIONALS

List five professionals in your network who might mentor young people or provide career exposure:

1. _____
2. _____
3. _____
4. _____
5. _____

NEXT STEPS

Pick three potential partners from your lists above and write down:

1. Why you think they'd be a good partner
2. What you'd ask them for (mentorship, space, funding, expertise)
3. When you'll reach out to them

SHARE THE MIC

"**I WANT BIPOC PARENTS TO KNOW** that your presence has power. Your voice deserves to be heard in every room where decisions are made about your children. Your wisdom, culture, and lived experience are strengths that help your children thrive."

—*Ayann*

"I met Rhona in Martha's Vineyard when a classmate connected us as I was just taking an Executive Director role at a financial literacy nonprofit for BIPOC high school youth. I shared our vision, and she shared that vision with her community of parents and colleagues. That fall, I had one-fifth of our high school scholars taking the train in from New Jersey to meet in person on Wall Street. That is the power of Rhona!"

—*Steve S., Wealth Management*

"Watching Rhona intentionally expose her children and other young Black and Latino youth to opportunities made me realize I could do the same thing. I created Cool Boys Read in 2007 specifically for Black and [B]rown boys who needed to see reading and learning as powerful, not just something forced on them in school.

For nine years, we built a community where boys competed in reading challenges, published their own stories in anthologies, created films, and took educational field trips—all while staying connected to their culture and identity. We served dozens of boys who might have fallen through the cracks of traditional programs that weren't designed with them in mind. My advice to anyone wanting to start something? You don't need a massive budget or a fancy organization. You need commitment, cultural understanding, and a willingness to show up consistently for young people who deserve to see themselves reflected in excellence."

—*Susan H., Founder of Cool Boys Read*

Need support?
Book a Complimentary Discovery Call
https://calendly.com/parentmatterz/early-start
Consulting-Discovery-Call

CHAPTER EIGHT
LOST, THEN FOUND—GUIDING TEENS THROUGH AN IDENTITY CRISIS

Your child is not lost. They're becoming.

But I know it doesn't feel that way when your once-bright teenager is suddenly withdrawn, unmotivated, or angry. When they stop talking to you. When their grades drop. When they say things like "I don't know what I want" or "Nothing matters" or "You just don't understand."

It's terrifying to watch your child struggle with their identity. To see them disconnect from everything you've worked so hard to build for them.

But here's what I've learned after twenty-five years of working with teenagers: An identity crisis isn't the end. It's the beginning.

It's the messy, uncomfortable process of figuring out who you are separate from who your parents want you to be. It's when young people start asking the hard questions: Who am I? What do

I believe? What do I actually want, not what everyone else wants for me?

As a parent, your job isn't to prevent an identity crisis. Your job is to guide them through it.

This chapter is about how to do that—how to stay connected when they're pulling away, how to support without controlling, and how to help them find themselves even when they feel completely lost.

THE TEEN WHO TRIED TO QUIT HIGH SCHOOL— THEN FOUND HIS WAY

My son wasn't a strong student. While most of his siblings were in advanced math classes in middle school, he wasn't. He struggled with self-confidence outside of sports and music. He had no clue about his future and honestly didn't care much about school.

During high school, he tried to quit multiple times. He was disconnected, unmotivated, and surrounded by peers who felt the same way. He'd come home, retreat to his room, and I could see him slipping further away from the version of himself I knew was in there.

I scheduled a meeting with his middle school principal before things got worse. The principal strongly suggested he take honors classes and eventually AP classes in high school. My son thought, *No way.* But the principal and I didn't accept that. He said, "The worst thing that could happen is you drop back to regular classes if you really can't handle it."

I also connected him to his high school's support services—tutoring, counseling, and a safe space to go when he felt overwhelmed. Those resources were a lifesaver.

But the real breakthrough came through mentorship. His high

school guidance counselor didn't just help him with schedules and transcripts. He became a family friend and mentor who coached him through life, college, and career situations. He was someone my son could talk to who wasn't his parent—and sometimes that's what a disconnected teen needs most.

I also made attending pre-college programs non-negotiable. He attended five programs over the years—one to four weeks each. He was furious with me. He wanted to stay home and relax like his friends. But those programs opened up his world. He met CEOs who looked like him doing big things. He built networking skills. He won awards. He traveled. And slowly, he started to see that his world didn't have to be as small as he thought.

In high school, he got exposed to theater and starred in a play. That confidence translated into other areas—he started a YouTube channel that now has over 70,000 followers. He used his newfound networking skills to land internships, and one summer program led to a full-tuition scholarship.

He studied abroad, played music with a jazz band in Europe, and graduated college. Today, he works in finance at a top firm and runs a business on the side. He even helps us financially.

But here's what matters most: He's no longer that disconnected teen who wanted to quit. He found purpose. And it didn't happen overnight—it happened through consistent mentorship, exposure, and refusing to let him think small.

WHY TEENAGERS GET "LOST"

Let's start by understanding what's actually happening.

Teenagers aren't trying to make your life difficult. They're going through one of the most intense developmental periods of their lives.

Here's what's happening in their brains and bodies:

- Their prefrontal cortex (the part that handles decision-making and impulse control) is still developing.
- They're experiencing massive hormonal shifts that affect mood and behavior.
- They're navigating increased social pressure, comparison, and identity formation.
- They're beginning to separate from their parents as part of healthy development.
- They're grappling with big existential questions for the first time.

Add to that the specific pressures facing Black and Brown teens:

- Navigating racism and microaggressions
- Code-switching between home and school/work environments
- Pressure to "represent" their entire community
- Limited representation in media, leadership, and professional spaces
- Higher rates of trauma exposure in under-resourced communities

No wonder they feel lost sometimes.

The "lost" phase isn't a sign that you failed as a parent. It's a normal, necessary part of adolescent development. The question isn't whether they'll struggle—the question is how you'll support them when they do.

THE THREE TYPES OF "LOST"

Not all identity crises look the same. I've seen three main patterns:

Type 1: The Withdrawn Teen

This is the kid who used to be talkative and engaged but has suddenly shut down. They stay in their room. They give one-word answers. They stop participating in activities they used to love.

What's really happening: They're overwhelmed. They don't know how to articulate what they're feeling, so they retreat.

Type 2: The Acting Out Teen

This is the kid whose grades are dropping, who's getting in trouble at school, who's pushing boundaries and testing limits. They're angry, defiant, or reckless.

What's really happening: They're expressing pain through behavior. They may be dealing with trauma, stress, or a crisis of identity that they don't have words for.

Type 3: The "I Don't Care" Teen

This is the kid who seems unmotivated about everything. They shrug when you ask about their future. They say things like "Nothing matters" or "I don't know what I want."

What's really happening: They're paralyzed by fear—fear of failure, fear of disappointing you, fear of making the wrong choice. So they choose nothing.

Your child might be one type, or a combination of all three. The point is: Their behavior is communication. Your job is to decode what they're really saying.

LOW MOTIVATION IS NOT LAZINESS

One of the biggest mistakes parents make is interpreting low motivation as laziness.

"They're just not trying."

"They don't care about their future."

"They're wasting their potential."

But low motivation is rarely about laziness. It's usually about one of these things:

- **Fear of failure:** "If I don't try, I can't fail."
- **Perfectionism:** "If I can't do it perfectly, why do it at all?"
- **Burnout:** "I'm exhausted from trying to meet everyone's expectations."
- **Depression or anxiety:** "I literally don't have the energy to care."
- **Lack of autonomy**: "Nothing I do feels like my choice, so why bother?"
- **Unclear purpose:** "I don't know why any of this matters."

If your child is unmotivated, don't shame them. Get curious. Ask: What's underneath this? What are they afraid of? What do they need that they're not getting?

RESISTANCE IS PROTECTION

When teenagers resist—when they push back against your advice, reject opportunities, or refuse to engage—it's often because they're protecting themselves.

They're protecting themselves from:

- Feeling like a disappointment

- Losing control over their own life
- Being forced into a path that doesn't feel like theirs
- Failing publicly
- Letting you down

Resistance isn't defiance for the sake of defiance. It's a defense mechanism.

When you meet resistance with more control ("You're going to do this whether you like it or not"), you escalate the power struggle. When you meet resistance with curiosity ("I'm noticing you don't want to do this. Can you help me understand why?"), you open the door to real conversation.

WHAT TEENAGERS NEED MOST

Here's what I've learned from working with teenagers who felt lost: They don't need you to have all the answers. They need you to create space for them to find their own.

Specifically, they need:

To be seen and heard. Not fixed. Not lectured. Just seen.

- **Autonomy within boundaries.** They need to feel like they have some control over their lives, even as you maintain appropriate limits.
- **Permission to struggle.** They need to know that it's okay to not have it all figured out. That struggling is part of the process, not a sign of failure.
- **Mentors who aren't their parents.** Sometimes they need to hear the same advice from someone else before they'll accept it. That's not a rejection of you—it's developmentally normal.

- **Purpose beyond achievement.** Grades and college applications aren't enough. They need to feel like their life has meaning beyond checking boxes.
- **A safe place to fail.** They need to know that if they try something and it doesn't work out, you'll still love them. That failure won't cost them your approval.

THE ROLE OF MENTORSHIP

Sometimes, the best thing you can do for a lost teenager is connect them with someone who isn't you.

I know that's hard to hear. You want to be the person who helps them. But teenagers are wired to separate from their parents during adolescence. That's healthy.

A mentor can say the exact same thing you've been saying for months, and suddenly your child listens. Not because you were wrong, but because they need to hear it from someone outside the parent-child dynamic.

Good mentors:

- Ask questions instead of giving advice
- Share their own struggles and failures
- Model healthy adulthood without pretending to be perfect
- Validate what the teen is feeling
- Hold them accountable with compassion
- Believe in them, even when they don't believe in themselves

If your child is lost, find them a mentor. A teacher, a coach, a family friend, a professional in a field they're curious about. Someone who can meet them where they are and walk with them through the fog.

THE IDENTITY EXPLORATION ACTIVITY

One of the most powerful tools I use with teenagers is the Identity Exploration Activity. It's simple, but it gets them thinking about who they are beyond what others expect them to be.

Here's how it works:

Step 1: Set the stage. Say something like: "I want to understand who you are right now—not who I want you to be, not who your teachers think you are, but who YOU think you are. There are no wrong answers."

Step 2: Ask them to complete these prompts:

- I feel most like myself when I'm...
- Something people don't know about me is...
- I wish people understood that I...
- I'm really good at...
- I'm curious about...
- I'm afraid of...
- I care deeply about...
- I want to be known for...

Step 3: Listen without judgment. Don't correct them. Don't give advice. Just listen. Their answers are data—information about who they are becoming.

Step 4: Ask follow-up questions. "Tell me more about that." "What draws you to that?" "When did you first realize that?"

Step 5: Affirm what you hear. "I hear you. Thank you for sharing that with me. I see you."

This activity isn't about solving their identity crisis. It's about showing them that you're interested in who they actually are, not just who you want them to be.

WHAT WOULD YOU TELL YOUR SIXTEEN-YEAR-OLD SELF?

Another powerful exercise is to have both you and your teen write letters to your sixteen-year-old selves. Then share them with each other.

Parent version: "What I wish I'd known at sixteen…"
Teen version: "What I want to remember about being sixteen…"
This exercise does two things:

1. It reminds your teen that you were once young and unsure too.
2. It gives your teen a chance to articulate what they're going through in a way that feels less vulnerable than direct conversation.

After you've both written your letters, read them aloud to each other. Then discuss:

- What surprised you about each other's letters?
- What did you relate to?
- What do you want to remember from this conversation?

This exercise creates empathy. It reminds both of you that identity formation is hard—and that you're on the same team.

WHEN PROFESSIONAL HELP IS NEEDED

Sometimes, a teenager's struggle goes beyond a normal identity crisis. Sometimes, they need professional support.

Signs that your child may need therapy or counseling:

- Persistent sadness or hopelessness
- Withdrawal from all friends and activities
- Significant changes in sleep or appetite
- Talk of self-harm or suicide (always take this seriously)

- Substance use as a coping mechanism
- Inability to function in daily life (not getting out of bed, not going to school)
- Extreme anxiety or panic attacks

If you see these signs, don't wait. Get help.

Therapy isn't a sign of weakness or failure. It's a tool. And sometimes, teenagers need a trained professional to help them process trauma, navigate mental health challenges, or develop coping skills.

As a parent, your job isn't to be your child's therapist. Your job is to get them the support they need.

THE LIGHT AT THE END OF THE TUNNEL

Here's what I want you to know: Most teenagers who go through an identity crisis come out stronger on the other side.

They figure out who they are. They reconnect with their purpose. They find their people. They build confidence. They grow.

But they need time. And they need you to hold space for them while they figure it out.

Your child is not lost. They're becoming. And your steady presence—your belief in them even when they don't believe in themselves—is what will guide them home.

ACTION ITEMS FOR PARENTS

1. Do the Identity Exploration Activity With Your Teen

Set aside an hour this week to go through the Identity Exploration prompts together. Create a safe, judgment-free space. Listen more than you talk.

2. Write Your "What I Wish I'd Known at Sixteen" Letter

Spend twenty minutes writing a letter to your sixteen-year-old self. Be honest about your struggles, fears, and what you eventually learned. Share it with your teen.

3. Connect Your Teen With a Mentor

Identify one adult (not you) who could mentor your teen through this season. Reach out to them this week and ask if they'd be willing to check in with your child regularly. Let us help.

4. Create One Non-Negotiable Connection Point

Establish one time each week where you and your teen connect—no agenda, no lectures, just presence. A weekly breakfast, a car ride, a walk. Protect that time fiercely.

5. Assess Whether Professional Support Is Needed

Honestly evaluate whether your teen is showing signs of clinical depression, anxiety, or trauma that requires professional help. If so, research therapists this week and schedule a consultation.

6. Practice Curiosity Over Control

The next time your teen resists something, resist the urge to force compliance. Instead, ask: "Help me understand what you're feeling right now." Practice getting curious instead of being controlling.

SHARE THE MIC

"**OUR SON WAS SUPPOSED** to start college, but during the entire college application process, he seemed uninterested and unmotivated. This attitude made us realize he wasn't ready to start college—and we certainly didn't want to waste our money.

It was a chance encounter with a friend that introduced us to the gap semester/year idea. After researching, we found a three-month program in East Africa. We had concerns about the safety and distance—East Africa felt far, and we weren't sure if the experience would help or damage his opportunities in college. But we overcame our concerns by having meaningful discussions with the program coordinators, talking to other families who had experienced the program, and getting assurances that the college he'd chosen would hold his spot and financial aid. Most importantly, while our son was scared of the "what ifs," he was open to the experience.

The beginning of his journey in East Africa (Tanzania, Uganda, Kenya) was rocky, with almost daily gut-wrenching phone calls of him wanting to come home. But once he settled in, the overall experience was awe-inspiring. He matured quite a bit. He needed time to breathe between the end of high school and the start of college.

The powerful thing? He graduated from college as an honor

student, which we truly believe was made possible by taking that gap semester. It launched his motivation to do well in college. And just as importantly, this experience gave him a love of travel, which is truly a gift he carries with him even today.

I highly recommend that you listen not only to the words your child says, but also to their nonverbal actions during the college process, to determine if a gap opportunity makes sense. For us, the long-term gifts of this experience make us know this was the right decision for our child, and we would do it again without hesitation. Gap semester/year programs come in many forms—just do your research and be open to a different pathway for your child as they embrace the journey to becoming independent young adults."

—*Patty B., Parent*

"When I was younger, I was frustrated. I wanted to be home relaxing like other kids, not participating in another program or attending another event. At times, it felt like my life wasn't my own—like I was just going through the motions of what my mom wanted for me, not what I wanted for myself.

That's what it feels like to be 'lost' as a teenager—you're trying to figure out who you are, separate from who your parents want you to be. But here's what I wish I'd understood then: My mom wasn't trying to control me. She was exposing me to options so that when I was ready to choose my own path, I'd actually have real options to choose from. The shift happened when I stopped resisting and started engaging. I explored different fields, met new people, and learned about myself along the way. What I'd tell other teens is this: It's okay to not know who you are yet. Try things. Some you'll love, some you'll hate. Both are valuable. Finding out what you don't want is just as important as finding what you do want. You're not lost—you're becoming."

—J.T., *Young Adult*

"Our daughter's freshman year of high school was both successful and promising. She earned a 3.5 GPA, sang in the school choir, and played sports. But during her sophomore year, we began noticing a decline in her grades and increasing drama among her friend group. Although she continued playing sports, her enthusiasm for school and learning faded. She surrounded herself with peers who were also unmotivated, and it was difficult for us to watch her potential slip away.

We sought therapy. We hired tutors. We engaged a college advisor who became a positive mentor in her life. Despite these supports, she began failing some classes and even stopped attending others. We also observed that a few teachers were not as supportive of students of color, which further contributed to her disengagement.

The hardest part for me as a parent was watching her withdraw and knowing that our usual strategies weren't working. We felt helpless.

Ultimately, we faced one of the most complex decisions we'd ever made as parents: transferring her to a small private school for her senior year. She was angry. For weeks, we drove to school in silence.

But after about a month, we began to see a shift in her mood and mental well-being. She connected with the one-on-one teaching style, felt seen and supported, and rediscovered her joy for learning. She excelled in music and film classes, regained her creativity, and graduated with a 4.0 GPA.

She completed her college degree with honors in contemporary music and most recently earned a certificate in post-production. She is now an intern for a production company in Southern California.

Looking back, I would not change a thing. Although the journey was challenging, it taught us to meet our daughter exactly where she was and to provide the support she needed. With the right environment, she was able to reclaim her confidence, reach her educational goals, and continue growing into her full potential."

—*Shelly C., M.Ed., Parent, Social Emotional Learning Specialist*

"I met Janiene when she arrived at Spelman College, and I had the privilege of watching her navigate that critical transition from teenager to young adult. What stood out was the foundation she came with—not just academically, but emotionally and socially. She'd been taught to advocate for herself, to build relationships with adults, and to ask for what she needed. But I also saw her wrestle with typical college-age identity questions: Who am I outside of my family? What do I really want? What are my values?

My approach was to create space for her to explore those questions without judgment. I didn't try to have all the answers. I asked questions, listened deeply, and reminded her that struggling with identity is normal and necessary. The trust between us grew because she knew I saw her as a whole person, not just a student to be fixed or molded. What I'd tell other adults who want to mentor teens: Your job isn't to prevent them from struggling. Your job is to walk with them through the struggle and remind them they're not alone."

—*Nikema W., Mentor*

"The hardest part of being a teenager right now is feeling like you're supposed to have everything figured out, but you don't. Adults ask, 'What do you want to be?' and I'm like, 'I'm 12—I'm still figuring out who I am.' What I wish adults understood is that we're trying.

Even when it looks like we don't care or we're being difficult, we're actually trying to figure out this whole life thing.

I feel most like myself when I'm around people who don't expect me to be perfect—when I can just be a kid without all the pressure. What helps when I'm feeling overwhelmed? When my mom shows up. Not with lectures or expectations, just shows up. Like when she takes time off work to spend time with us, even though she's busy. That makes me feel like I matter, like I'm not just another thing on her to-do list. I think that's what all teenagers need—adults who show up, not just with advice, but with presence."

—*Kai M., Age Twelve, Seventh Grade*

Need support?
Book a Complimentary Discovery Call

https://calendly.com/parentmatterz/early-start
Consulting-Discovery-Call

CHAPTER NINE
FROM EXPOSURE TO EXECUTION

Exposure opens doors. Execution walks through them.

I've seen it happen too many times: A young person gets exposed to an incredible opportunity—a mentorship, an internship, a program that could change their trajectory—and then they don't follow through.

They don't submit the application on time. They don't show up consistently. They don't send the thank-you email. They don't do the work required to turn the opportunity into an outcome.

Exposure without execution is just a nice experience. It's potential that never becomes reality.

This chapter is about closing that gap—teaching your child not just to recognize opportunities, but to act on them with discipline, follow-through, and persistence. Because, at the end of the day, success isn't about who gets the most opportunities. It's about who executes on the opportunities they get.

FROM THE BUS STOP TO CORNELL: ARLENE'S JOURNEY FROM EXPOSURE TO EXECUTION

I met Arlene at the bus stop when she was in third grade and my daughter was in second grade. Her mom was newly remarried, new to the block, and expecting Arlene's first little brother.

We became more like sisters than neighbors. Over the years, Arlene's mom literally said to her: "Whatever Miss Rhona says to do, you do it."

One day, her mom asked me, "Why do you care so much for others not related to you?"

I explained that I've been blessed. My children have had multiple moms—wherever we lived, whatever the season, God always put someone or a village in my life to help me carry the invisible load. It could have been as simple as carpools, so I could get to work early or stay late, or someone to help me navigate life, work, marriage, single motherhood, job transitions, being underpaid, and making ends meet. I will never forget each and every one of these women. Many of their voices are heard on these pages—my village literally rocks.

Now that I'm the most stable I've ever been in my adult life—not worrying about my safety from exes, my car being repossessed, the lights being turned off, or being locked out of my apartment—I have a cup full enough to pour into someone else. God moved us to the same block for a reason. It didn't matter that our language, culture, or country of origin wasn't the same. We became family.

Arlene did swim lessons, karate, and everything else my kids did. She even followed my son to his magnet high school. When she got there, I told her about the issues I'd had with that school, and she created space for change—even inviting me as a guest speaker.

She was a true star in our Girl Scout troop. Everywhere I lived, if I wanted my daughters to be Girl Scouts, I was told there were no available troops. So I became a leader in North Carolina, California, and New Jersey in order for my three daughters to participate.

My last troop in New Jersey was amazing. It consisted of 10 Black and Brown girls who got exposed to every career, mentor, and opportunity out there. This was my training ground pre-Parent Matterz. Arlene was shining like a diamond. She was the close-in-age big sister my youngest needed.

THE TURNING POINTS

Arlene was a star student in middle school. I took her and the troop to a STEM event at Cooper Union College in NYC. She definitely loved science, and everyone loved her teacher, Mr. Hickey. But something clicked at that day-long event for middle school students. Even though she was gifted in science, she wasn't sure she loved it enough for a career, after all.

In seventh grade, I took the troop to several legal events. One was *The Color of Justice*—all Black and Brown female lawyers and judges. Powerful. I made each of them go introduce themselves and find a mentor. They were terrified.

In eighth grade, Arlene was asked to do a report for school on someone from her culture. She chose Jennifer Lopez. The teacher asked her to choose someone else outside of entertainment. She reluctantly chose Supreme Court Justice Sonia Sotomayor, after someone suggested her.

It changed the game for her. Her interest in law made her light up.

WHAT MADE ARLENE DIFFERENT

Here's what set Arlene apart from other students who had similar exposure, but didn't follow through: She executed. She didn't just show up to events—she took action afterward. She majored in Law in high school. She pursued great internships. She applied the lessons from every mentor she met.

And she stayed connected to her village. Even when things got hard, she leaned on the people who believed in her.

WHERE SHE IS NOW

Four years ago, Arlene couldn't have imagined where she is today. As a first-generation college student with little understanding of what lay ahead, the path wasn't easy. But she graduated from Cornell University, becoming the first in her family to attend and complete a degree at an Ivy League institution.

During commencement, she had the distinct honor of serving as the Degree Marshal for the ILR School—a moment that symbolized not only personal achievement but also the growth, resilience, and leadership she developed over four years.

In her own words:

"These past four years have been some of the most challenging of my life, and I am deeply thankful for the village that helped me persevere. To the friends, mentors, and chosen family who consistently believed in me—thank you for reminding me of my potential, especially when I struggled to see it myself.

Most importantly, I owe everything to my mother. Your unwavering support and example have shown me what it means to be a strong, independent woman who leads with both excellence and heart. As a proud Dominican woman entering an underrepresented field, I carry your lessons with me every step of the way.

While I'm incredibly proud of this milestone, my journey is just beginning. J.D. loading..."

Today, Arlene works for JPMorgan Chase as an HR analyst. And she's already planning her next move—law school.

Arlene is like my sixth child. And watching her journey from that bus stop in third grade to Cornell's commencement stage reminds me why this work matters. Exposure plants the seed. But execution—showing up, following through, staying connected—is what makes the dream real.

THE EXPOSURE-EXECUTION GAP

Here's what I've learned after decades of working with young people: Exposure creates possibility, but execution creates outcomes.

The students who succeed aren't necessarily the ones with the most talent or the most resources. They're the ones who:

- Show up consistently, even when it's inconvenient.
- Follow through on commitments, even when they're hard.
- Ask for help when they need it, instead of giving up quietly.
- Take feedback without getting defensive.
- Do the unglamorous work that no one sees.
- Stay focused on long-term goals, even when short-term distractions tempt them.

These aren't innate qualities. These are skills. And parents can teach them.

But here's the problem: Many parents focus all their energy on creating exposure and forget to teach execution. They get their kid into the program. They make the connection. They open the door. And then they assume their child will naturally know what to do next.

But most kids don't. They need to be taught how to execute.

WHAT EXECUTION ACTUALLY LOOKS LIKE

Execution isn't flashy. It's not the exciting part. It's the daily, consistent habits that turn exposure into outcomes.

Here's what execution looks like in practice:

Following Through on Applications

You found the perfect summer program for your child. Great. Now, are they actually filling out the application? Are they meeting deadlines? Are they proofreading their essays? Are they following up if they don't hear back?

Execution means sitting down with them, creating a timeline, breaking the application into manageable steps, and holding them accountable to deadlines. I remember two distinct occasions that could have changed my children's trajectory—both times we almost missed critical deadlines.

The first was an application to one of the top magnet public high schools in the country. We had done all the work but never hit submit after a final edit. We were riding a roller coaster at an amusement park when it hit me—the deadline was midnight that night. We called my oldest daughter and she pulled up the application and hit submit for her brother. He got in.

The second near-miss was a scholarship that came with mentorship and an all-expenses-paid week-long trip to DC. I was at a function when I remembered—another midnight deadline. I got off the dance floor to call home and say, "Wake your brother up and remind him to submit the application." He got the prestigious scholarship that usually only went to students attending HBCUs, even though he was attending a Predominantly White Institution (PWI).

Both deadlines were midnight. Both times we almost missed them. Both opportunities changed their life.

Showing Up Consistently

Your child got into the mentorship program. Wonderful. Now, are they showing up to every session? Are they arriving on time? Are they prepared?

Execution means building routines around their commitments, helping them manage their schedule, and teaching them that consistency matters more than talent.

Communicating Professionally

Your child shadowed a professional for a day. Excellent. Did they send a thank-you email? Did they follow up a month later to share what they learned? Did they maintain the relationship?

Execution means teaching them how to write professional emails, when to follow up, and why relationships require ongoing investment.

Doing the Unglamorous Work

Your child wants to be a doctor. Great. Are they doing the daily studying required to excel in science classes? Are they volunteering at a hospital, even when it's boring?

Execution means helping them understand that the glamorous

goal requires unglamorous work, and building the discipline to do that work even when no one's watching.

Taking Feedback and Adjusting

Your child applied for an internship and didn't get it. Did they ask for feedback? Did they revise their resume? Did they apply again to other opportunities?

Execution means teaching them that feedback is a gift, rejection is data, and persistence is more valuable than perfection.

WHY SMART KIDS DON'T ALWAYS EXECUTE

Some of the smartest, most talented kids I've worked with struggle with execution. Here's why:

They're used to things coming easily. When something requires sustained effort, they give up because they interpret difficulty as a sign they're not good at it.

They're perfectionists. They don't start because they're afraid they won't do it perfectly. So they procrastinate or avoid altogether.

They lack structure. They have big goals, but no system for breaking those goals into daily actions. So they feel overwhelmed and do nothing.

They don't see the connection between daily habits and long-term outcomes. They think success happens in big, dramatic moments, not in the boring, consistent work no one sees.

They've never been held accountable. No one taught them that commitments matter, deadlines are real, and follow-through is non-negotiable.

These are all fixable. But parents have to teach execution explicitly—not just assume their child will figure it out on their own.

THE PARENT AS COACH MINDSET

Think of yourself as a coach, not just a cheerleader.

Cheerleaders celebrate. Coaches hold folks accountable.

Cheerleaders say, "You can do it!" Coaches say, "Here's exactly how to do it, and I'm going to check in with you to make sure you're following through."

Here's how to coach execution:

Set Clear Expectations

Don't just expose your child to an opportunity and hope they figure it out. Sit down with them and clarify expectations.

"You've been accepted into this program. Here's what's expected of you: Show up on time, complete assignments, communicate professionally with mentors. If you commit, you follow through. Are you in?"

Create Structure

Big goals feel overwhelming. Break them into small, actionable steps.

Instead of: "Apply to 10 scholarships this semester."

Try: "Every Saturday morning, we spend one hour working on scholarship applications. By the end of the month, you'll have submitted three."

Hold Them Accountable (With Compassion)

Check in regularly. Ask: "Did you follow through on what you committed to?" If not, don't shame them—help them problem-solve.

"What got in the way? What support do you need? How can we adjust so you can succeed?"

Model Execution Yourself

Your child is watching how you follow through on your own commitments. Do you meet deadlines? Do you do what you say you'll do? Do you persist when things are hard?

You can't coach execution if you're not modeling it.

Celebrate Effort, Not Just Outcomes

When your child follows through—even if the outcome isn't perfect—celebrate that. Execution is the behavior you want to reinforce.

"I'm proud of you for showing up every week, even when you didn't feel like it. That's discipline."

THE GOAL-PLANNING FRAMEWORK

One of the most powerful tools I use with young people is a simple goal-planning framework. It turns vague dreams into concrete action plans.

Here's how it works:

Step 1: Identify the Goal

Ask: "What do you want to achieve in the next six to twelve months?"

Be specific. Not, "I want to go to college," but, "I want to get accepted to three colleges with strong biology programs."

Step 2: Identify Why It Matters

Ask: "Why does this goal matter to you? What will achieving it give you?"

This is the motivation that will sustain them when execution gets hard.

Step 3: Break It Into Milestones

Ask: "What are the major steps required to reach this goal?"
Example:

- Research 10 colleges with strong biology programs (by October).
- Visit three campuses (by December).
- Complete college applications (by September).
- Submit the FAFSA (by October).

Step 4: Break Milestones Into Weekly Actions

Ask: "What do you need to do this week to make progress?"
Example:

- This week: Research two colleges and add them to the list.
- Next week: Schedule campus visit to first college.

Step 5: Identify Obstacles and Support

Ask: "What might get in your way? What support do you need to succeed?"

Example obstacles: Procrastination, not knowing how to write essays, feeling overwhelmed

Example support: Weekly check-ins with parent, essay writing workshop, application tracker

Step 6: Set Check-In Dates

Schedule regular check-ins to review progress. Weekly or bi-weekly works well.

This framework transforms "I want to go to college" into a concrete plan with accountability built in.

WHEN EXECUTION BREAKS DOWN

Even with support, execution sometimes breaks down. Here's what to do:

Identify the Breakdown Point

Where exactly did things fall apart? Was it starting? Following through? Maintaining consistency? Asking for help?

Don't Shame—Troubleshoot

"What happened?" is more useful than "Why didn't you do it?"

Get curious. Was the goal too big? Did life get in the way? Did they lose motivation? Did they not know how to ask for help?

Adjust and Try Again

Maybe the goal needs to be smaller. Maybe they need more structure. Maybe they need external accountability.

Execution is a skill. It improves with practice. Don't give up after one failed attempt.

Consider Whether They're Ready

Sometimes a young person isn't ready for a particular opportunity. That's okay. It's better to wait until they have the maturity and discipline to execute, than to push them into something they'll fail at.

I received a last minute invite to take five high school girls to a week long S.T.E.A.M. event at Google in NYC. I had 48 hours to find young women available to ride the bus and train with me at 6 a.m. to the incredible opportunity. I found five middle school girls and they were probably not 100% ready, but as college seniors now, they still remember the people, great free food, and getting mentored by Google executives and the esteemed global AI executive Dr. Loretta Cheeks.

THE LONG GAME

Execution is what separates exposure from impact.

Your child might attend a hundred programs, meet a hundred mentors, and visit a hundred colleges. But if they don't execute—if they don't follow through, do the work, and persist through challenges—those experiences won't translate into outcomes.

Teaching execution is teaching your child how to be someone who finishes what they start, who keeps commitments, and who does the hard work required to turn potential into reality.

That's the skill that will serve them for the rest of their lives.

As my son entered high school as a freshman, I was given unsolicited advice from other parents: "Don't let your son take Honors English with Ms. Wright."

Thank God I'm not the parent who tries to choose my kids' teachers.

First of all, it's almost impossible. Second, I wanted my kids to have experiences with many different teaching styles and personalities. In the real world, they won't get to choose their bosses, I thought. They needed to learn how to navigate with many different types of people.

I remember parents as early as elementary school trying to make this happen. I will say I'm grateful for many of my children's teachers, but especially Mrs. Simpson. My last three had her for fourth grade. She came from corporate after retiring young and brought all that real-world knowledge to her students. She was extra heavy on discipline with the boys, and I loved it. We still spend time with her when we can. She was a game changer for my children.

Going back to Ms. Wright: My son was placed in her class by the way.

She called me on a Sunday in September, at the beginning of the school year. My youngest and I were on the Ferris wheel in Toys R Us in midtown Manhattan when the phone rang. Ms. Wright said, "Please don't take him out of my class. He may not get an A or B, but if you let me work with him after or before school, I can teach him how to take tasks and break them down into bite-size, digestible pieces. He will carry this skill throughout life."

My son loved going to see Ms. Wright when he didn't have baseball or music practice. She taught him life skills and how to maneuver when under pressure or feeling like a task was too monumental.

Ms. Wright, Mrs. Simpson, and so many educators like Dr. Small (their former principal) poured into my children and helped them gain the confidence they needed in life.

I beg you to partner with your child's teachers and administrators for a powerful outcome. Send an email before school starts introducing your child, letting them know their strengths and gifts, and listing areas where they need help developing. That partnership for a child is magical.

ACTION ITEMS FOR PARENTS

1. Use the Goal-Planning Framework With Your Child

Sit down with your child and walk through the six-step goal-planning framework. Pick one meaningful goal (college, internship, scholarship, skill) and create a concrete action plan together.

2. Create a Weekly Execution Check-In

Schedule fifteen minutes every week to check in on your child's progress toward their goals. Ask: "What did you commit to? Did you follow through? What support do you need?"

3. Identify One Area Where Your Child Needs Accountability

Is it submitting applications on time? Showing up consistently to a program? Following up with mentors? Pick one area and create a system to help them execute.

4. Teach Professional Communication

Have your child write one professional email this week—to a teacher, a mentor, or a program coordinator. Review it together before they send it. Teach them how to be clear, respectful, and direct.

5. Model Execution in Your Own Life

Choose one commitment you've been putting off and execute on it this week. Let your child see you follow through. Talk about how you overcame resistance or stayed disciplined.

6. Celebrate One Example of Your Child's Follow-Through

Notice and name when your child executes. "I'm proud of you for submitting that application a week early. That's what execution looks like."

"PARENT AS COACH" CHECKLIST

Use this checklist to assess whether you're coaching execution effectively:

CLARITY

- ☐ Have I clearly communicated what's expected of my child?
- ☐ Does my child understand why this commitment matters?
- ☐ Have we broken big goals into small, actionable steps?

STRUCTURE

- ☐ Does my child have a system (calendar, checklist, tracker) to stay organized?
- ☐ Have we scheduled regular check-ins to review progress?
- ☐ Have we identified potential obstacles and planned for them?

ACCOUNTABILITY

- ☐ Am I checking in consistently on commitments?
- ☐ Am I holding my child accountable with compassion (not shame)?

- ☐ Am I addressing breakdowns quickly instead of letting them slide?

SUPPORT

- ☐ Does my child know they can ask me for help without judgment?
- ☐ Have I connected them with resources (mentors, tutors, programs) they need?
- ☐ Am I celebrating effort and progress, not just outcomes?

MODELING

- ☐ Am I demonstrating execution in my own life?
- ☐ Am I following through on commitments I make to my child?
- ☐ Am I showing them what persistence looks like?

SHARE THE MIC

"**I WAS GIVEN** an incredible opportunity through my mother's nonprofit, Teaneck Comes Together. She provided me with an internship that gave me exposure to the nonprofit space and opportunities to serve my community. But exposure alone wouldn't have changed my trajectory—I had to execute. I had to show up consistently, learn the work, build relationships, and apply what I was learning. What helped me stay committed was watching my mother's work ethic. She was balancing a full-time job as a social worker while building and running a nonprofit. She showed me what execution looks like: doing the unglamorous work, following through on commitments, persisting even when you feel unappreciated or face obstacles.

I didn't just observe her organization—I participated in it, served through it, and learned from it. That hands-on experience taught me how to turn exposure into action. The result? I founded my own nonprofit, Teaneck Stays Together, to continue serving my community. Exposure gave me the vision. Execution made it real. My advice to young people: Don't just attend the program or accept the opportunity. Do the work. Follow through. Apply what you learn. That's how you turn potential into impact."

—*Khalil W. Stanford Scholar Athlete and Attorney*

"I can't truly say I had a plan when we started the college process with our older son. All we knew was that he was a high school sophomore, and the college process needed to begin.

We were blessed to be told about a program called Operation Link Up (OLU) that would forever change his life. My son did not like going to the OLU meetings, but I didn't let him quit. I knew that his participation in OLU was what granted him acceptance to Syracuse University, which probably would not have happened if we had let him stop the program.

By the time his younger brother entered high school, OLU was phasing out, so we had to rely on our previous experience to guide him. I told him to trust my guidance in the process. He did, and got accepted into competitive schools like Marist and Lehigh. He chose Cornell.

During both my sons' senior year, I started staying on top of them to have college applications submitted by mid-November. My husband and I said no to activities that would interfere with them doing their best on the applications. We said yes to activities that would enhance their high school experience and applications—or that were required for school, extracurriculars, and church.

What surprised me most about teaching execution? My tenacity was rewarded with the tightest hug from my son on his graduation day. He said, 'Thanks for not letting me quit OLU!'

Everything we learned during those experiences became the foundation for starting College CAFE™, whose motto is 'Know More, Pay Less.'

My advice to parents starting this journey: Take a deep breath. Each child is different, and so will be their paths. Observe your children to see what they gravitate to—that may indicate their future careers. Don't be afraid to say No or to challenge them to try new things. It may be the most obscure, random opportunity that allows them to shine and become the amazing person they were meant to be.

Create a support system for yourself and your children. Be organized and start the process as early as eighth grade. It's never too early to start preparing for your child's future.

During the COVID-19 lockdown, as the year changed from 2020 to 2021, I started posting quick videos that caught the attention of a local nonprofit. The president approached me to moderate a webinar series. In a future episode, the topic was scholarships.

A few years prior, I had met a nurse whose daughter was in nursing school at a local university. This young lady had spearheaded a fascinating process when it came to scholarships. She sought them out on her own and ensured that no opportunity passed her by. This allowed her to graduate with very little debt.

What made her stand out? She was proactive. She didn't wait for opportunities to come to her—she went looking for them. She researched. She applied. She followed through. And she listened to guidance from adults who had been through the process before.

It goes to show that proactive research and effort can significantly impact educational financing. But a student must also be willing to listen. You are just starting out, so listening to the guidance of adults who came before you must be foremost in your plan for success.

Execution isn't just about working hard. It's about working smart, staying consistent, and being willing to learn from those who've already walked the path."

—Dr. Ketsia S., Parent and Founder of College CAFE™

"My mom made me attend a program for boys of color, introducing them to coding. I was actually at another program when they had an orientation, and my mom went in my place. All I could think was, 'I hope she hates it so I don't have to go.' I felt like she was a lot and always doing the most with us—especially me.

She was upset after the orientation because she didn't see many Black and Latino boys. Other Brown boys were taking full advantage. She was on a mission from that point on to get as many young men in the program, including me, whether they were interested in coding or not.

The premise of the program was learning to get comfortable with failure. Coding is more about failure than success. Looking back now, it was a lot of professional development. They also taught us how to get out of our comfort zone. One day, we walked the streets of New York asking random questions like, 'Do you have a postage stamp?' For a shy guy like me, that was a lot. The program allowed us to learn to fail forward.

It ended each summer with a gala in NYC where we got to meet board members and donors, and then a fundraiser in the Hamptons on the estate of one of our first Black billionaires. My mom, a native New Yorker, volunteered to be a chaperone. She had never been to the Hamptons.

I met famous people at the event, like Van Jones. He grabbed my phone and made me take a selfie when he visited my booth. He said, 'Your mom will be mad if we don't take this selfie.' Each student in the cohort got to exhibit the app they built and demo it at their booth, seeking investors, advice, or mentors.

This was life-changing for my mom and me. She networked like crazy. I was still shy. My mom had to force me to go to the gala in NYC. Both my parents joined me, and that helped a lot. My mom and dad had a great time. It was wild to see them networking and spending a lot of time with attorney Loida Lewis, the widow of Reginald Lewis.

The one opportunity I missed—and regret now—was the chance to spend the day at Google with the Black and Brown engineers. I woke up with red eyes. My mom didn't force me to go. I definitely regret it now.

She said something I'll never forget: 'Parenting is like knowing when to put your foot on the gas, the brakes, or coast in neutral.'

What made execution hard for me? Honestly, I was shy. I didn't always see the value in what my mom was pushing me toward. I felt overwhelmed sometimes.

What changed? Watching my parents show up for me. Seeing them network and support me at events. Realizing that the opportunities I was resisting were actually opportunities other kids would greatly appreciate..

What would I tell my younger self about follow-through? Stop resisting. Trust your parents. Show up even when you don't feel like it. You'll regret the things you didn't do way more than the things you tried and failed at."

—*Software Engineer*

Need support?
Book a Complimentary Discovery Call
https://calendly.com/parentmatterz/early-start
Consulting-Discovery-Call

CHAPTER TEN
THE LEGACY PLAN—BUILDING YOUR CHILD'S FUTURE BY DESIGN

Your child's future doesn't happen by accident. It happens by design.

Not your design. Theirs. But your job is to give them the tools, exposure, experiences, and guidance they need to design a life worth living.

This final chapter is about stepping back and looking at the big picture. What are you building? What legacy are you creating? What will your child thank you for ten, twenty, thirty years from now?

And most importantly: What do you need to do today to make that future possible?

This is your legacy plan.

FAITH, REST, VISION, AND ACTION

Over the past 25+ years of raising five children while building programs, organizations, and movements, I've learned that sustainable parenting requires four pillars: faith, rest, vision, and action.

Let me break that down.

Faith

Faith isn't just religious (though for me, it is). Faith is the belief that your child's future is bigger than their current circumstances. It's trusting that the seeds you're planting today will bloom, even if you can't see the results yet.

Faith is what keeps you going when your teenager is struggling, when opportunities fall through, when you've invested everything and it feels like nothing is working.

Faith says: I don't see the outcome yet, but I trust the process. I trust my child. I trust that what I'm doing matters.

Without faith, you burn out. With faith, you persist.

Rest

I learned this lesson the hard way. After the birth of my fifth child, I developed a neurological illness that left me unable to walk, stand, or even hold my baby. I was forced to rest for six months. I hired help I couldn't afford. I eventually filed for bankruptcy.

But that rest saved my life.

It taught me that motherhood should be cherished, not survived. That you can't pour from an empty cup. That taking care of yourself isn't selfish—it's essential.

Now I take breaks every six weeks. I rest intentionally. I model for my children that your well-being matters, that rest is productive, that you can't build a legacy if you're running on fumes.

Parents who don't rest become resentful, exhausted, and ineffective. Parents who rest become sustainable, present, and powerful.

Vision

You need a vision for what you're building. Not a rigid plan that doesn't allow for adjustments, but a guiding vision that keeps you focused.

My vision has always been: Build warriors and great humans. Give them the most phenomenal survival toolbox I can create, so they can leave the world better than they found it.

That vision guided every decision. Every program I enrolled them in. Every conversation we had. Every opportunity I pursued for them.

Your vision might be different. But you need one. Because without a vision, you're just reacting. With a vision, you're designing.

Action

Faith, rest, and vision mean nothing without action.

You have to do the work. Make the phone calls. Fill out the applications. Show up to the meetings. Have the hard conversations. Hold your child accountable. Invest the time, energy, and resources required to build the future you envision.

Action is where legacy is built. Not in what you intend to do, but in what you *actually* do.

WHAT WILL YOUR CHILD THANK YOU FOR?

Twenty years from now, what will your child thank you for?

They won't thank you for being perfect. They'll thank you for being present.

They won't thank you for never making mistakes. They'll thank you for owning your mistakes and growing from them.

They won't thank you for giving them everything they wanted. They'll thank you for giving them what they needed—even when it was hard.

Here's what I believe they'll thank you for:

Exposure

"Thank you for showing me what was possible before I even knew to dream it."

Exposure to careers, cultures, experiences, and people expanded their sense of what they could become. It interrupted limiting beliefs and opened doors they didn't know existed.

High Expectations with High Support

"Thank you for believing I could do more than I thought I could—and for supporting me in getting there."

You didn't just push them. You equipped them. You held them to a high standard while giving them the tools, guidance, and encouragement to meet it.

Permission to Fail

"Thank you for letting me try things, fail, and try again without losing your belief in me."

You created a safe space for them to take risks, make mistakes, and learn from failure without fearing your disappointment or rejection.

A Village

"Thank you for surrounding me with people who poured into me, believed in me, and showed me different ways to live."

You didn't try to be everything to your child. You built a village of mentors, teachers, coaches, and community members who invested in their growth.

Rest and Self-Care

"Thank you for showing me that taking care of yourself isn't selfish—it's necessary."

You modeled what it looks like to rest, set boundaries, and prioritize your well-being. You taught them that they don't have to sacrifice themselves to be successful.

Faith and Resilience

"Thank you for teaching me that setbacks aren't the end—they're part of the journey."

You modeled resilience. You showed them how to bounce back from disappointment, loss, and failure. You taught them that faith carries you through hard seasons.

BUILDING YOUR OWN NETWORK

You don't have to run a nonprofit to do this work. You don't have to organize events or create programs. But you can absolutely be part of the solution by building your own grassroots network.

Here's how:

Start by identifying the parents in your circle who are actively looking for opportunities for their kids. These are your people. Create a group chat, a Facebook group, an email thread—whatever works. Commit to sharing resources, opportunities, and information.

Connect with people in your community who work with youth. Coaches, teachers, librarians, youth pastors, community center staff. Let them know you're looking for opportunities for your child and other kids in the neighborhood. Ask them to keep you in the loop.

When you find a good program, don't keep it to yourself. Tell everyone. Post about it. Send texts. Make announcements at church or community events. Assume that if you didn't know about it, others don't either.

Be the connector. If you know a parent whose child is interested in engineering, and you know an engineer, make the introduction. If you hear about a scholarship opportunity, think about which families in your network would benefit and reach out to them directly.

Show up to community events—not just as a participant, but as someone actively building relationships. Learn names. Exchange numbers. Follow up after the event.

Don't wait for someone else to organize things. If you see a need, fill it. Start a monthly meetup for parents in your neighborhood.

Create a carpool system for kids to get to programs. Host an info session in your living room.

The point is this: We can't rely on institutions to reach every family. We have to do it ourselves. We have to become the bridges that connect kids to opportunity.

THE LEGACY LETTER

One of the most powerful exercises I recommend to parents is writing a Legacy Letter to your child.

This isn't a letter you'll send tomorrow. It's a letter you write to your future child—the adult they'll become—reflecting on what you hope they'll carry with them from their childhood.

Here's how to write it:

Start with gratitude: "I'm so grateful I got to be your parent."

Reflect on who they are: "You are [qualities you see in them]."

Share your hopes: "I hope you know [what you want them to remember]."

Acknowledge your imperfections: "I didn't always get it right. I [specific mistakes]. But I hope you know I [your intentions]."

Affirm their future: "I believe you will [your vision for them]."

End with love: "No matter where life takes you, I'm proud of who you're becoming."

This letter isn't for them—it's for you. It's a way to clarify what matters most, what you're building toward, and what you want your child to remember about your parenting.

You can keep it private, or you can share it with them when the time is right.

THE YOUTH OPPORTUNITY TIMELINE

One of the tools I've used with countless families is the Youth Opportunity Timeline. It's a planning sheet that maps out what opportunities, experiences, and milestones you want to prioritize at different stages of your child's development.

Here's the framework:

Ages 0-12: Foundation Building

Focus: Exposure, curiosity, trying new things
Opportunities to prioritize:

- Extracurriculars (sports, arts, clubs)
- Community service or volunteering
- Exposure to different careers (career days, shadowing parents/relatives)
- Building basic life skills (cooking, budgeting, time management)

Ages 13-15: Exploration and Skill Development

Focus: Identifying interests, building skills, developing independence
Opportunities to prioritize:

- Summer programs or camps in areas of interest
- Leadership roles in school or community
- Part-time jobs or internships
- Mentorship relationships
- College campus visits (even if just for exposure)
- Explore vocational and technical programs

Ages 16-18: Execution and Preparation

Focus: College/career readiness, goal-setting, follow-through
Opportunities to prioritize:

- College applications, scholarships, FAFSA
- Advanced courses (AP, dual enrollment, vocational training)
- Internships or work experience in field of interest
- Building professional skills (resume writing, interviewing, networking)
- Financial literacy and planning

Ages 19-22: Independence and Growth

Focus: College success, career exploration, self-sufficiency
Opportunities to prioritize:

- Internships, co-ops, research opportunities
- Study abroad or travel experiences
- Building a professional network
- Mental health and wellness support
- Career planning and goal refinement

Ages 23-25: Launch and Legacy

Focus: Career establishment, financial independence, giving back
Opportunities to prioritize:

- First job or graduate school
- Professional development and skill-building
- Financial planning (saving, investing, debt management)
- Mentoring younger students
- Building community and staying connected to roots

This timeline isn't rigid. Your child's path might look different. But it's a guide—a way to think strategically about what opportunities to pursue when.

DON'T LET THEM WATCH MORE THAN ENOUGH TV

One of the notes in my outline for this chapter said: "More than enough TV."

Let me tell you what I mean by that.

I'm not anti-TV. I'm not saying your child can never relax or have downtime. But I am saying this: If your child has time to binge-watch an entire series, scroll TikTok for hours, or play video games all weekend, they have time to invest in their future.

Time is the most valuable resource your child has. How they spend it determines their trajectory.

Are they spending their time consuming, or creating?

Are they scrolling, or studying?

Are they watching other people's success, or building their own?

I'm not asking you to turn your home into a productivity boot camp. But I am asking you to be intentional about how your child uses their time.

If they have free time, encourage them to:

- Read books that expand their thinking
- Learn a new skill (language, instrument, coding, cooking)
- Volunteer or serve their community
- Work on a passion project
- Build something, create something, contribute something

The young people who succeed aren't the ones who had more time. They're the ones who used their time differently.

FINAL THOUGHTS: YOU ARE ENOUGH

If you've read this far, you care. You're investing. You're showing up.

That matters.

You don't have to be perfect. You don't have to have all the answers. You don't have to do everything I've outlined in this book.

But you do have to be present. You do have to be intentional. You do have to believe in your child's potential and invest in their future.

Here's what I want you to know:

You are enough.

Your love is enough. Your effort is enough. Your commitment to showing up, even when it's hard, your love is enough.

Your child doesn't need a perfect parent. They need you—the imperfect, trying, learning, growing you.

So take a deep breath. Give yourself grace and feel the warm hug from me. And keep going. Because the legacy you're building—one conversation, one opportunity, one act of faith at a time—is going to change your child's life.

And twenty years from now, they're going to **THANK YOU** for it.

ACTION ITEMS FOR PARENTS

---

1. Write Your Legacy Letter

Set aside 30 minutes this week to write a Legacy Letter to your child. Use the prompts in this chapter. Keep it private, or share it when the time feels right.

2. Create Your Youth Opportunity Timeline

Use the framework in this chapter to map out opportunities you want to prioritize for your child at each stage (ages 10–12, 13–15, 16–18, etc.). Adjust based on where your child is now.

3. Audit Your Child's Time

Track how your child is spending their free time for one week. Then sit down with them and discuss: Is this how you want to spend your time? What would you change?

4. Schedule Your Next Rest

If you haven't rested in months, schedule a break. A day off. A weekend away. An afternoon to yourself. Model rest for your child.

5. Revisit Your Vision

What's your vision for what you're building with your child? Write it down in one sentence. Share it with your partner or a trusted friend. Use it to guide your decisions.

6. Celebrate What You've Built

Look back at how far your child has come. Write down five things they've achieved, learned, or grown in because of your investment. Celebrate it.

LEGACY LETTER EXERCISE

USE THESE PROMPTS to write your Legacy Letter:

Dear [Child's Name],

I'm writing this letter to you as the adult you'll become. Right now, you're [age], and I see so much potential in who you're becoming.

I'm so grateful I got to be your parent because...

You are [qualities you see in them: brave, curious, kind, resilient, creative, etc.]...

I hope you know...

I didn't always get it right. I [specific mistakes or regrets]. But I hope you know I [your intentions behind your choices]...

I believe you will [your vision for their future: impact, contribution, joy, success]...

No matter where life takes you, I want you to remember...

I'm proud of who you're becoming.

Love,

[Your Name]

YOUTH OPPORTUNITY TIMELINE PLANNING SHEET

_____

USE THIS SHEET to plan strategic opportunities for your child at each stage:

AGES 0–12: Foundation Building

Top three opportunities I want to prioritize:

1. _____
2. _____
3. _____

AGES 13–15: Exploration and Skill Development

Top three opportunities I want to prioritize:

1. _____
2. _____
3. _____

AGES 16-18: Execution and Preparation

Top three opportunities I want to prioritize:

1. _____
2. _____
3. _____

AGES 19-22: Independence and Growth

Top three opportunities I want to prioritize:

1. _____
2. _____
3. _____

AGES 23-25: Launch and Legacy

Top three opportunities I want to prioritize:

1. _____
2. _____
3. _____

SHARE THE MIC

"**NOW THAT I'M AN ADULT,** what I appreciate most is that I was raised in a house full of love and genuine respect. Not every household has that, and I didn't fully understand how rare and valuable that was until I got older.

As a kid, I didn't understand why my parents would tell me to just be quiet and listen—especially when I had so much to say. But now that I'm older, I've learned the power of observation. Sometimes the best thing you can do is listen, watch, and absorb what's happening around you before you speak. That lesson has served me in college, in internships, and in every professional space I've entered.

The legacy my parents left me is being an independent woman who is extremely educated and humble. They taught me that intelligence means nothing if you don't stay grounded. They showed me how to work hard, pursue excellence, and still treat people with kindness and respect.

What will I carry forward to my own children? Being grateful and nice to everyone. You never know who you'll meet, and connections are everything. My parents modeled that for me every day—the way they treated people, the way they built relationships, the way they opened doors for others. That's the kind of parent I want to be.

I didn't always understand their approach when I was younger, but now I see it clearly. They weren't just raising me—they were preparing me for a world that doesn't always make space for people who look like me. And because of them, I know how to navigate that world with confidence, grace, and humility."

—*Sydni H., Montclair State University Senior*

"My vision as a parent has always been guided by intentionality—making sure my children excel both academically and socially, while also growing into well-rounded individuals. My non-negotiables included prioritizing quality time over work or distractions, respect as a foundation in our home, consistency in routines to provide stability, accountability for their choices, and instilling faith and integrity as guiding values.

Twenty years from now, I hope my sons will say that I was present, that I gave them opportunities to explore the world through sports, music, and travel, and that I equipped them with the tools to navigate life with confidence.

For parents just starting this journey, my advice is to be intentional at every stage. Support your children step by step, be present without overthinking, embrace imperfection, listen to them, and recognize their individuality. Each child is unique, and parenting is about meeting them where they are."

—*Tresha C Parent, ; Founder and CEO of Inspired Horizon Collectives*

"By the time I met Rhona Vega in 2018, a few people had already told me about her. They would say, 'She's doing the same work as you' or something similar. It felt like we already knew each other in that first meeting. I knew we were destined to work together when, at the 2019 Bergen County NAACP Luncheon, Jeff Carter, the chapter president at the time, asked us to stand and said, 'These two women are having an impact assisting students in Bergen County with the college process.'

When Rhona first approached me requesting assistance with Junior Jump Start, I couldn't say no. Just hearing the inspiration behind the program was enough for me to provide my assistance and expertise. It's even more inspiring to see how the students and parents react to the different speakers who take time to engage with them, both in person and virtually. One summer we had two cohorts working simultaneously, but we made it work. I often say that we're the 'yin and yang' of college preparedness.

Rhona has an unmatched energy and zest for students' successes! No matter where she is, it becomes an opportunity to connect with people who will have an impact on the students she works with later. Rhona turns random conversations into alliances where students can attend impactful conferences for free. Initial meetings with people from various careers become automatic invitations to join one of the speed networking sessions during a Junior Jump Start boot camp.

It's also amazing to see students walk through the Expos that Rhona started a few years ago. She hosts them at local high schools and has expanded to reaching students as far away as Martha's Vineyard. When you see the excitement on their faces, talking to college and career representatives—some of whom they might not have ever encountered—you know that her countless early mornings were not in vain. Every program she puts together builds on her foundation of blood, sweat, and tears, supported by the experiences she gained with her five children. Students walk away knowing that the future holds many possibilities for success!

I'm grateful that we met, and I have learned so much from her! College CAFE™ has grown in some ways thanks to its partnership with Parent Matterz on different occasions. 'Iron sharpens iron,' as the saying goes. If you are around Rhona Vega, you will grow and accomplish much, even if you don't want to! I know she will continue assisting many students in achieving their post-high school dreams. Keep up the great work, Queen Rhona Vega!"

—*Dr. Ketsia S., EdD, RN, CSN, CHES, CIHWC;*
Founder, College CAFE™

Need support?
Book a Complimentary Discovery Call

https://calendly.com/parentmatterz/early-start
Consulting-Discovery-Call

EPILOGUE
YOUR TURN

If you've made it this far, you're not just reading anymore—you're deciding.

You're deciding whether to keep doing what you've always done, or to step into something different. You're deciding whether to wait for opportunities to find your child, or to go hunt them down yourself. You're deciding whether to parent in survival mode, or to parent with strategy, intention, and a vision for what's possible.

I wrote this book because I've lived it. I've been the mom working multiple jobs, stretched too thin, wondering if I was doing enough. I've been the mom who didn't know what she didn't know. I've been the mom who had to figure it out on her own because no one was showing me the way.

But I also learned something powerful along the way: **You don't have to do this alone.**

The strategies in this book—exposure, village-building, college readiness, execution, legacy planning—they work. I've seen them work for my own five children. I've seen them work for hundreds of students and families who've walked through Parent Matterz programs. I've watched kids who were written off become college graduates, scholarship winners, corporate leaders, and community change-makers.

But here's the truth: **None of it happens by accident.**

It happens because parents like you decide that average isn't good enough. That "getting by" isn't the goal. That your child deserves more than what the system is offering them.

It happens because you refuse to let your child be invisible.

WHAT HAPPENS NEXT?

This book gave you the blueprint. Now it's time to build.

You don't need to do everything at once. You don't need to be perfect. You just need to start.

Pick one action item from one chapter and do it this week. Just one.

Schedule one college visit. Research one scholarship. Connect your child to one mentor. Attend one informational session. Have one honest conversation with your teen about their future.

One action creates momentum. And momentum creates change.

YOU DON'T HAVE TO FIGURE THIS OUT ALONE

When I started Parent Matterz, it was because I wished someone had handed me a roadmap. I wished someone had told me what programs existed, what scholarships were out there, how to navigate the college process, and how to advocate for my kids without losing my mind.

Now I'm that someone for you. If you're feeling overwhelmed, our team is here to help.

Here's how you can stay connected and keep building:

1. Schedule a Free Parent Consultation

Not sure where to start? Feeling overwhelmed? Let's talk. I offer free 15-minute consultations to help parents figure out their next steps.

Whether your child is in seventh or twelfth grade, whether they're thriving or struggling, let's create a plan that works for your family. Get access to our network and database of resources, enrichment programs, upcoming events, and tools to help you navigate your child's educational journey. Whether you're starting in middle school, scrambling in senior year, or you're somewhere in between, there's something here for you.

Scan the QR code or https://calendly.com/parentmatterz/early-start-consulting-discovery-call

2. Subscribe to the Parent Matterz YouTube Channel

I post videos regularly with practical tips, step-by-step guidance, scholarship alerts, and real talk about the challenges parents face. Think of it as your weekly dose of encouragement and strategy. Search "Parent Matterz" on YouTube and hit subscribe.

Email: parentmatterz@gmail.com

Subject line: "I want to raise kids who will thank me later"

3. Join the Parent Matterz Community

Follow us on Instagram and Facebook (@ParentMatterz) for daily tips, success stories, scholarship alerts, and a community of parents who are doing this work alongside you. You're not alone in this journey—there's a whole village waiting for you.

4. Attend a Youth Opportunity Expo or host one in your area with the help of Parent Matterz

Come to one of our Youth Empowerment and Opportunity Expos. These events bring together colleges, programs, mentors, and resources all in one place so you and your child can explore opportunities face-to-face. Follow us on social media or on Eventbrite for upcoming dates.

5. Bring our career and college readiness programs like Junior Jump Start to your school, local Boys and Girls Club, YWCA, YMCA, sorority or fraternity chapter, local Jack and Jill, church or community center.

Our signature college and career readiness boot camp prepares high school students for life after graduation. It's where exposure meets execution. If your child (middle or high schooler) needs a jump start on their future, this program is for them. Learn more by scheduling a strategy call at (**https://calendly.com/parentmatterz/parent-matterz-strategy-call**) or scan the QR code.

6. Share This Book

If this book helped you, pass it on. Lend it to another parent. Gift it to a friend. Recommend it to your child's school. Post about it on social media. Tag me (@ParentMatterz), so I can celebrate with you. Request your school district order copies for all guidance counselors and have your local library order it.

The parents who need this book the most are often the ones who don't know it exists. Help me reach them.

A FINAL WORD

I STARTED THIS BOOK BY SAYING THAT EXPOSURE IS OXYGEN. And it is.

But here's what I want you to remember as you close this book and step back into your life:

You are the oxygen.

You are the one who opens doors. You are the one who makes the call. You are the one who says, "My child deserves this opportunity," and refuses to take No for an answer.

You are the one who builds the village, creates the plan, and believes in the vision, even when your child doesn't see it yet.

You are the one who shows up tired, stretched thin, and overwhelmed—and does it anyway.

That's not just parenting. That's legacy work.

And twenty years from now, when your child looks back on their life and sees how far they've come, and THANKS YOU, they're going to trace it back to this moment. The moment you decided to do things differently. The moment you said, "Not on my watch."

So here's my challenge to you:

Don't let this book sit on a shelf.

Don't let this be one more thing you read and thought was inspiring, but never acted on.

Pick one chapter. Pick one strategy. Pick one action item.

And do it. Because your child is counting on you. Not to be perfect. Not to have all the answers. But to show up and fight for their future the way only you can.

You've got this.

And if you ever doubt that—if you ever feel like you're doing it wrong, or not doing enough—come find me. Send me an email, leave a direct message (dm) on Instagram. Leave a comment on YouTube. Show up to an event.

Let me remind you that you're not alone. That you're doing better than you think. And that every single thing you're doing right now is planting seeds for a harvest you'll see years from now.

Keep going, QUEEN. Keep going, KING.

Your child's future is worth it.

And so are you.

With love and unwavering belief in you,

Rhona Vega
Chief Dreamer Parent Matterz
Mom of Five | Keynote Speaker | Your Success Coach

P.S.—If you take one action after reading this book, post about it on social media and tag me (@ParentMatterz). I want to celebrate with you. I want to see the moves you're making. And I want other parents to know that change is possible.

Let's build this movement together.

One parent. One child. One opportunity at a time.

ADDITIONAL RESOURCES

This resource page includes tools, organizations, and websites referenced throughout this book to support your child's educational journey.

CONNECT WITH PARENT MATTERZ

Founded by Rhona Vega to provide families with access to opportunities, programs, scholarships, and resources for youth success.

YouTube: Search "Parent Matterz" on YouTube for The Power Of Exposure episodes.

Instagram & Facebook: @ParentMatterz for internships, scholarship alerts, and practical guidance

Schedule a Strategy Call: https://calendly.com/parentmatterz/parent-matterz-strategy-call

Programs Offered:

- Junior Jump Start Boot Camp (college and career readiness for middle and high school students)

- Youth Opportunity Expos (connecting students with colleges, organizations, and resources)
- Scholarship alerts and application support
- Mentorship and enrichment programs

COLLEGE PLANNING & FINANCIAL AID

FAFSA (Free Application for Federal Student Aid)

Website: https://studentaid.gov

The gateway to federal grants, loans, and work-study programs. FAFSA opens October 1st every year. Create your FSA ID early and complete your application as soon as possible—some aid is first-come, first-served.

Key reminder: FAFSA is FREE. Never pay anyone to complete it.

College Board

Website: https://collegeboard.org

Resources for SAT registration, test preparation, college planning timelines, and scholarship search tools.

Khan Academy

Website: https://khanacademy.org

Free SAT prep, academic resources, and test-taking strategies.

Advanced College Planning

Website: https://advancedcollegeplanning.net/the-complete-college-planning-timeline/

Comprehensive college planning timeline referenced in this book for step-by-step guidance through the college process.

COMMUNITY ORGANIZATIONS MENTIONED

College CAFE™

Motto: "Know More, Pay Less." A college planning organization focused on helping families navigate the college process and reduce education costs.

Teaneck Comes Together & Teaneck Stays Together

Community-focused nonprofits providing youth programming, internships, and service opportunities in Teaneck, NJ.

Math Adventure and Word Play

A FREE tutoring program (K-12) that ran for more than twenty years, founded by Pat Phillips Walser and Dr. Ardie Walser. A model of accessible education for all families.

FEATURED PROFESSIONALS

Kamora Freeland

Website: https://www.kamorafreeland.com/pressfeatures
Professional featured in this book whose work and journey offer valuable insights.

TIPS FOR FINDING LOCAL RESOURCES

As emphasized throughout this book, many of the best opportunities exist in your own community. Here's how to find them:

- **Contact your local library** – Ask about free SAT/ACT prep, college planning workshops, and youth programs.
- **Check with community centers** – Many offer after-school programs, mentorships, and enrichment activities.
- **Connect with faith-based organizations** – Churches, mosques, synagogues, and temples often have youth coordinators and scholarship funds.
- **Research local nonprofits** – Search "[your city] youth programs" or "[your city] college access programs."
- **Join parent groups** – Create or join a group chat, Facebook group, or email list with parents committed to sharing opportunities.
- **Build your village** – Identify coaches, teachers, business owners, and professionals in your network who can mentor or open doors for your child.
- **Attend community events** – School board meetings, youth sports games, neighborhood festivals—these are where you meet other families and learn about resources.

SCHOLARSHIP SEARCH STRATEGIES

As discussed in Chapter 5:
- Start searching in eighth or ninth grade to learn what qualifications scholarships require.
- Apply broadly – don't just chase big national scholarships; local ones often have less competition.

- Treat scholarship applications like a part-time job.
- Reuse and adapt essays (but always proofread and change names!).
- Don't ignore small scholarships – they add up.
- Look for scholarships from: local organizations, Greek organizations, alumni associations, community foundations, professional associations, and corporations.

STAY CONNECTED & SHARE OPPORTUNITIES

The grassroots network is powerful. Every time you learn about an opportunity, scholarship, program, or resource, share it with at least three other families. Don't assume they already know.

Tag @ParentMatterz on social media when you take action on strategies from this book. Let's build this movement together—one parent, one child, one opportunity at a time.

"The opportunities are out there. They're just not advertised to us. This resource page is your starting point. Now go find them, apply for them, and share them with other families who need them."

—*Rhona Vega, Founder of Parent Matterz*

ABOUT THE AUTHOR

Rhona J. Vega is an award-winning and highly sought-after public speaker and consultant. She is an expert on college and career readiness, and has connected thousands of historically excluded youth to life-changing resources.

She is the Chief Dreamer of Parent Matterz, an organization that helps youth connect to resources, find their passion, and turn it into a paycheck. She hosts Youth Empowerment Expos at schools and on Martha's Vineyard and has created life changing workshops for middle schoolers to college students on college and career readiness. She also hosts "Blueprint to Success" workshops and speed networking events to introduce youth to career exploration and mentors.

Rhona has been featured on a GEICO radio commercial on the Black Entertainment Network, Fox5, and NBC4 NY. She has also been featured in the Bergen Record in NJ and the Martha's Vineyard Times.

Early Start Consulting is the one-on-one holistic success coaching program that Rhona created to help coach individual students and families.

www.ingramcontent.com/pod-product-compliance
Lightning Source LLC
Chambersburg PA
CBHW051122160426
43195CB00014B/2308